# Dalí

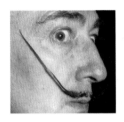

# Dalí

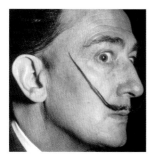

Linde Salber
translated by Anne Wyburd

HAUS PUBLISHING · LONDON

First published in Great Britain in 2004 by
Haus Publishing Limited
26 Cadogan Court, Draycott Avenue
London SW3 3BX


Originally published under the title *Salvador Dalí*
in the series 'rowohlt monographien'
Copyright © 2004 by Rowohlt Verlag GmbH, Reinbek bei Hamburg
The author would like it to be known that the original German-language
edition was written in the present tense and in short sentences. To conform to
the house style of the *Life & Times* series of monographs, the English
translation is given in the past tense and the author's interpretations in the
field of the psychology of art have been greatly simplified.
The moral right of the author has been asserted.

English translation © Anne Wyburd
A CIP catalogue record for this book is available from the British Library

ISBN 1-904341-75-6 (paperback)
ISBN 1-904341-76-4 (hardback)

Designed and typeset in Garamond by John Miles
Printed and bound by Graphicom in Vicenza, Italy

Front cover: photograph of Salvador Dalí courtesy of Lebrecht Picture Library
Back cover: courtesy of Lebrecht Picture Library

# Contents

# SALVADOR DALÍ

'If you were to tell me that all this could be calculated mathematically – chaos, confusion, cursing and the rest – so that it was always possible to calculate everything and reason would remain paramount, I believe man would *deliberately* go mad, so as to be devoid of reason and therefore able to rely on himself.'

Dostoevsky:
*Notes from Underground*

## Self-dramatisation from the beginning: the exaltation of his early years (1904-1922)

Anyone following in Dalí's tracks will soon realise that everyone else has been there before. For example, in Figueres – the artist's birthplace – the curtain goes up before your eyes each morning, half-an-hour before the Teatro-Museo Dalí opens. There will be twelve buses in the car park and groups of school children sitting at the feet of monstrous monuments, waiting to be let in. The queue, including a remarkable number of young people, will be over 50 metres long – and not just in the summer. Even in the dead season tourists from all over the world fill the village of Cadaqués, hidden away on the coast, where the Dalís spent their summers.

What are they looking for? A close-up view of a hero of perversity? His surreal extravaganzas? The effect of the landscape which he had 'dalified', the cliffs he turned into myths, the sun, the floppy clocks, the melting cheese? One certainly hears plenty of 'Oh my God', and 'breathtaking' and 'terrific' to describe the Cadillac in the courtyard, its effect heightened by Ernst Fuchs's *Queen Esther* sculpture floating like an angel above it and with Wagner's music breathing a soul into it.

On 11 May 1904 Salvador Felipe Jacinto Dalí y Domènech was born in Figueres in Catalonia, on the Mediterranean coast of Spain. In his own words: *On the thirteenth day of May 1904 Don Salvador Dalí y Cusí, born in Cadaqués, Province of Girona, 41 years old, married, notary, resident at Calle de Monturiol 20, appeared before Senor Miguel Comas Quintana, the honourable local judge and his secretary, Don Francisco Sala y Sabria, to register the birth of a child and informed the afore-mentioned judge that the said child had been born at fifteen minutes to nine o'clock on the eleventh day of the same month and that he had been named Salvador Felipe y Jacinto, that he was the legitimate son of himself and his wife, Doña Felipa Dome Domènech, aged 30, born in Barcelona and living with him. The paternal grandparents were: Don Galo Dalí Vinas, born in Cadaqués, deceased, and Doña Teresa Cusí Marco, born in Rosas; the maternal grandparents were: Doña Maria Ferrés Sadurne and Don Anselmo Domènech Serra, born in Barcelona. The witnesses were: Don José Mercader, born in La Bisbal, Province of Girona, tanner, resident Calzade de Los Monjes 20, Cadaqués, and Don Emilio Baig, born here, musician, resident in Calles de Perelada 5, both being of age.*[1]

This is like a Biblical recitation of names and places, which always sounds surreal, mixed with the dry tones of the legal contracts which as a notary Salvador's father handled daily. It continues in this Biblical vein: *Let all the bells ring!… Look! Salvador Dalí has just been born.*[2]

The new Salvador was the second son of Don Salvador Dalí y Cusí (1872-1952) and his wife Felipa Domènech Ferrés (1874-1921) and replaced the first Salvador, who was born on 21 October 1901 and died on 1 August 1903 at the age of only 22 months, exactly nine months and ten days before the painter's birth.

So 'Salvador II' started as something of a substitute. Out of this precarious position grew his plan: to prove to his parents, himself and the whole world that he was in fact 'original' and to avoid at any cost appearing to be a repetition, *so as always to be the first.*[3] Accepted standards, conventions and normality must be cast aside. With exaltation and by breaking through barriers Salvador invented his own remarkable sphere of activity. Once he had succeeded in seizing on the chance to extrapolate his own actions ad absurdum he felt himself somehow unique. He had to prove that he was a genius; otherwise Salvador II could have been absorbed into the unfinished history of Salvador I – the history of a dead boy. Visiting his grave must have scared the child.

*At the age of six I wanted to be a cook, at seven I wanted to be Napoleon and my ambition has been steadily rising ever since.*[4] So he wrote at the age of 37– an adult looking back on his childish dreams with amused detachment. Yet his ambition did continue to soar and in 1972 he drafted an 'Opera Poem' entitled 'Being God'.

A second look at his autobiography, *The Secret Life of Salvador Dalí,* makes one realise that it should be taken seriously, as the fictionalised personal history of an artist who has made a deep impression on 20th century aesthetics. With an eye sharpened through psychoanalysis and the typically Spanish characteristic found in Don Quixote, he invented a character who finds himself in a (literally) ex-centric situation. Referring to the thesis of the psychoanalyst Otto Rank set out in his *Birth Trauma* (1924), Dalí described his antenatal experience: *The colours of my intra-uterine paradise were hellish – red, orange, yellow and bluish, the colours of flames of fire; above all it was warm, motionless, soft, symmetrical, padded and sticky. I already felt that all pleasure and all enchantment lay there before my eyes and the most wonderful and striking illustration of this was two fried eggs without their frying pan [...].*[5]

This 'account', if one does not dismiss it as merely a fantasist's comic invention, could be read as the introductory agenda for a deranged aesthetic programme or, in simpler terms, as describing the visual experience, pictorial subjects and painting method of the famous Spanish surrealist Salvador Dalí. The words indicate that his artistic vision was not a kind of fad but relied on a quasi biological necessity pre-experienced in the effect of pressure *(the closed fists on the eye-sockets in the characteristic foetal position)*[6] and after birth he could repeat it at any time by pressing a finger on his pupils.

Dalí located the foundations of his own artistic history in his mother's womb. It was his mother, too, who made little Salvador's transition from paradise to earthly life as effortless as possible. If one accepts his own version and that of his sister Ana Maria, this child was denied a civilising upbringing with its built-in sanctions. No-one scolded him for any of his childish caprices – getting dirty, making a mess, daubing surfaces with paint, wetting himself, pestering, shamming, daydreaming, fibbing, insatiably demanding – and not even for his tantrums, which could be very violent. When competition with his father for his mother's love reached a climax – for instance when he pretended to have a fit of coughing during meals – his mother always took his side. When she woke the little boy in the morning, her first question was: 'My sweet, what would you like? My sweet, what do you want?'7 She seems to have overlooked all the wilfulness of this child who was bent on pleasing himself. Salvador was happiest when dressing up in his royal robe with crown and sceptre, so it is hardly surprising that he thought it absolutely intolerable to have to go to school and suddenly find himself being treated like an ordinary child among other children. He simply did not function like a social being; he regarded school as a challenge to him to assert his 'specialness'.

*When I was seven my father decided to take me to school. He had to use force and with a great effort dragged me by the hand, while I screamed the whole way and made such a commotion that all the shopkeepers in the streets we went through came out to look at us.*8 In actual fact Salvador was four when that happened and therefore at a moment of great difficulty in sharing his parents' affection with his newborn sister Ana Maria. Like all children of his age he saw his uniqueness being threatened and now his overpowering father wanted to drive him out to school. *By then my parents had* *taught me two things: the alphabet and how to write my name. At the end of my first school year they discovered to their dismay that I had completely forgotten both. My teacher was Señor Trayter, which sounds like the Catalan word for omelette, and he was really an extraordinary man in every way.*[9] Esteban Trayter Colomer was an art fanatic who, according to Dalí, had built into his house all kinds of Romanesque and Gothic sculptures and windows from old churches.

Dalí as a boy

*I spent […] my first year at school with the poorest children of the town, which I believe was very important for the development of my congenital megalomania. I did in fact grow more and more used to considering myself, the rich child, as a precious, delicate being, completely different from the ragged children around me. I was the only one who […].*[10] There follows a recitation of his special features: Salvador smelled of perfume, he had silver buttons on his jacket and shoes, his thermos flask was wrapped in a silken cloth embroidered with an emblem, and so on. *While I withdrew into silence, the other children raged around as though possessed by whirling demons, […] thereby exhibiting the usual hereditary feeble-mindedness which lies dormant in every healthy biological specimen and forms the normal nutrient for the practical, animal development of the 'principle of reality'. How far removed was I, in contrast, from this development of a 'practical principle of*

*reality'! In fact, I was at the opposite pole. [...] 'Practical conduct'
was my enemy [...].*[11]

During lessons Salvador paid no attention to what was going
on in class but gazed out of the window instead, watching the
colours of the two cypress trees outside changing with the light as
the day wore on, or lost himself in contemplation of a
reproduction of François Millet's *Angelus* which hung in the
classroom. He only learnt to write properly when he was given an
*exercise book with silk paper*[12]. *I certainly made no progress on the
steep and thorny path of arithmetic and had no success with the
loathsome and arduous workings of multiplication. [...].*[13] But the
boy was making his own aesthetic observations while sunk in
childish dreams. On a school excursion he found a nut from a
plane tree which became 'his' monkey, and invented a
significance for it in his daydreams. A little Russian girl, whom
his teacher had shown him in a stereoscopic picture, merged in
his mind with a live girl he had seen sitting by a fountain and he
built her into stories which fascinated him for a long time. Years
later in his autobiography he identified her with his wife Gala.

Dalí's mother's fervent love helped to give him the courage to
uphold his 'visions' in the face of ordinariness throughout his life.
She herself had artistic leanings. His grandmother Maria Anna
Ferrés was widowed very young, when his mother was only 13,
and when she set up a workshop to produce artefacts her young
daughter had helped her to design them. Doña Felipe made little
figurines out of candle-wax for her son, and saw from his earliest
creations that he had inherited her interest.

Dalí's sister Ana Maria reported on their mother's
partisanship. When little Salvador once scraped away the red
paint of the balcony table and called the white shapes which
emerged his ducks and swans, she remarked with enthusiasm:
[...] 'When he says he'll draw a swan, he draws a swan; and when
he says he'll do a duck, it's a duck [...].*[14] A child's delight in

Portrait of my Father, 1925 (oil on canvas).
Museu d'Art Modern, Barcelona, Spain

asserting that his fantasies are reality does not always meet with such understanding in adults, especially when it is damaging pristine possessions in the process. The visionary transformations and interpretations of reality so dear to children are usually sacrificed to the realism adults generally regard as absolute.

A close friend of Dalí's father, Pepito Pitxot, watched the boy as closely and enthusiastically as the 'mothers' – a term which included his mother's sister, Catalina ('La Tieta') and his grandmother, who had both been living with the Dalí family since about 1908. Pepito Pitxot's brother Ramón was a Catalan painter well known at the time, a friend of Pablo Picasso who had worked for a while in his studio in Paris. Ramón Pitxot's pictures were among the first originals to attract Salvador's attention. At an exhibition in the Edison cinema in Figueres in 1913 Dalí's father bought the still life *Pomegranates* from the painter.

One day, when his mother asked him the usual question about what he wanted, Salvador replied: […] *one of the two washing rooms in the attic […]. And next day I was allowed to take possession of the laundry, which was so small that it was almost entirely filled by the stone tub, […] but the extremely limited dimensions of my first studio perfectly corresponded to my memories of intra-uterine joys […]. I put my chair in the tub and laid the long wooden board […] flat across it, so that it half covered the tub. That was my worktable! […] the walls were covered with pictures I had painted on the lids of hatboxes made of very pliable wood, which I stole from my aunt Catalina's clothes shop.*[15]

Up there the child nursed his visions and fantasies of grandeur. His sister was not allowed in. *Once I reached the attic I realised I had once again become unique. […] The whole panorama as far as the bay of Rosas seemed to belong to me and to depend on my gaze.*[16] The only books and objects he took up with him were those which could inspire and stimulate his daydreams. Imagining himself the ruler of the world above the roofs of Figueres, Salvador found that by painting he could give expression in intensified hallucinatory images to his childishly sensuous relationships with things and people and in this way to confront with them the insipidity cultivated in his school.

The efforts of society and culture to gather people and things together into a generality, so as to introduce order, control and system into individual chaos, have another effect, because as a result singularity, uniqueness, chance and individuality are disparaged as being merely subjective or simply empirical. There are exceptions to this, one of which is childhood. In our early years we do not live in concepts or constructions (for which speech with its grammatical and sentence structure prepares us instinctively, and therefore unawares), but follow our sensuous taste for what we perceive in any given situation, which can lead to an explosion of ideas and perspectives - mainly unconnected and ephemeral. Childish behaviour and experience give an impression of being chaotic, wild, wilful, intuitive and creative; they seem in more or less spectacular ways to be the opposite to adult life, which is generally organised by rules and regulations. Another exception is art, which provides scope for bringing to life elementally conceived relationships between things and people.

According to his sister, Dalí was given his first box of oil paints in 1914 by the German painter Siegfried Bürrmann[17], but the amateur painter Juan Salleras from the village of El Sortell, on the sea near Cadaqués, had already entered his life. Like Dalí's father, Salleras was a close friend of Pepito Pitxot, whose wealthy landowning family loved art and music and kept an open house. They rented holiday cottages to friends, among them the Dalís, who lived right on the shore at Es Llanes, in a small converted stable which they later bought. Dalí's father loved this area where he had spent his childhood. It seems that six-year-old Salvador spent hours on end watching their neighbour Juan Salleras at work.

Although he was so absent-minded at school, Salvador 'studied' works of art in his laundry retreat on his own initiative. *I brought the complete volumes of 'Art Govens' up to my laundry; these little monographs, which my father had given me when I was quite small, were among the greatest influences on my life. By spending days looking at them I came to know by heart all these reproductions of old masterpieces, which I had been familiar with from earliest childhood. [...] I could go on forever recounting what I experienced in my washtub, but one thing is certain – that it was there my sense of humour got its first pinch of spice. I was already beginning to try out my facial expressions, combining a merry twinkle of the eyes with a slightly wicked smile. Dimly, vaguely, I knew I was watching myself playing the role of a genius. Oh Salvador Dalí! Now you know: if you play the genius, you will become one.*[18]

Dalí was an actor reporting on the beginnings of self-dramatisation and inviting the reader to participate in the strange leaps of his psyche. The make-believe turned into a pose which was reflected as reality in the eyes of the people who were important to him, above all his mother. The particular charm of his autobiography lies in the fact that the adult Dalí manages to describe his childhood mentality in such vivid style and language that its exaltations and ecstasies correspond exactly to his artistic mentality. The autobiography has been criticised as not being a factual account, but that is not so, for Dalí is putting into words the 'spiritual' facts which usually perish in the child's process of becoming civilised.

On coming down from his Olympus into the reality he shared with other people, Salvador found himself in an extraordinarily intense moment of transition: *At dusk I came out of the laundry, and this was my favourite moment! The smooth, soundless flight of swallows had already gone by with that other, rival flight of the awkward, swaying bats; I waited a little longer for that delightful moment when I took off my crown which had become so tight that a sharp stabbing in my temples had turned into a headache. [...]. Wracked with pain, I recited aloud such bombastic and over-accentuated speeches that I was saturated with a fantastic, passionate tenderness for myself. [...] The turmoil of megalomania then reached such heights of egocentric delirium that I felt I had climbed to the summit of the most unattainable stars [...]; in such a moment a peaceful, reasonable stream of tears flowed over my smooth face and soothed my soul. For a while I had already felt something small, moist and bizarre in my caressing hand. With surprise I saw that it was my penis.*[19]

Dalí was describing a condition in which his inner life

corresponded neither to the outer world nor to a biological sexual urge, but in which behaviour, experience, nature and technical achievements were indissolubly blended and intensified. He was describing the greed for life of this child who wanted to realise everything and the opposite of everything all at once, the key being the concepts of orgiastic multiplicity and promiscuity of desire. Nevertheless he repeatedly stressed his deeply felt need for order, format, discipline, plan and strictness.

He found both aspects realised in art – that is, in the luminous paintings of Ramón Pitxot, which he looked at during breakfast during a holiday at the Pitxots' country house at El Moli de la Torre (The Mill Tower). *For me those breakfasts marked the discovery of French impressionism, the school which in fact made the greatest impression on me in my whole life [...]. My eyes could not take in all that I wanted to see in those dense, formless splashes of colour which seemed to have been sprayed at random onto the canvas in a carefree and very capricious way. But if one looked at them from a certain distance with narrowed eyes, there dawned an unbelievable miracle of vision through which this jumble of colours organised itself into pure reality. Air, distances, sudden bursts of light, all the phenomena in the world rose out of chaos! [...]. In the dining room there was a jug with a glass stopper through which everything looked impressionistic.*[20]

Once, when he ran out of canvas, he used a discarded door as a painting surface. *On it I began to paint a picture which had been haunting me for several days – a still-life with a huge pile of cherries. I shook a whole basketful onto my table to use as a model. The sun streaming through the window fell on the cherries and fired my inspiration. [...] I decided to paint the picture with just three colours applied directly from the tube. [...]. Each cherry – three strokes! Whoosh, whoosh, whoosh – light, dark, highlight; light, dark, highlight ... In no time at all I had matched the rhythm of my work to the sound of the mill – clack, clack, clack ... clack, clack, clack*

Dalí at highschool

*...clack, clack, clack ... My picture developed into a fascinating game of skill.*[21]

When he found woodworm holes in the door he prised the worms out with a needle and put cherry stalks in. *I had already done four or five of these bizarre, crazy substitutions, when I was surprised by Señor Pitxot.*[22] *He couldn't help murmuring to himself 'That shows genius!' Some hours later at lunch he said: 'I have decided to speak to your father about finding you an art teacher.' The idea horrified me and I answered furiously: 'No! I don't want anyone to teach me, because I am an "impressionist" painter!' I didn't know the exact meaning of the word 'impressionist' but my answer seemed to me incontrovertibly logical. Señora Pitxot was completely flabbergasted and burst into loud laughter.*[23]

That was probably in 1916 when Salvador was just twelve and had passed the entrance exam for the Instituto in Figueres – a public academy which prepared pupils for the equivalent of the baccalauréat, the qualification for entering university. Dalí's father, who was implacably severe, had insisted that his son should stop spending his free time after primary school with the Christian Brothers in Els Fossos and face the demands of a normal school career. He also enrolled him in the private college of the Marist Brothers. At that time in Spain many children of ambitious parents were put through two schools. To his parents' surprise Salvador came home at the end of the year with 'good', 'excellent' and 'outstanding' on his school report.

In the Instituto Dalí met the art master Pitxot had wanted for him, Juan Nuñez Fernandez, a draughtsman and copperplate engraver who occasionally painted in oils. He was also Director of the Figueres Art School, where Notary Dalí enrolled his son in evening classes [24] and where after only a year he was awarded a 'diploma of honour'. Teacher and pupil were important to each other, both wanting to stimulate and intensify their enthusiasm, knowledge and proficiency in the sphere of art, and both liking to think that they belonged to the community inhabited by the great artists of the past.

Salvador quickly made progress. He often spent the evening at Nuñez's house, *where he explained to me the mysteries of chiaroscuro and the 'wild strokes' (that was his expression) of an original Rembrandt etching which he owned. I always came away greatly stimulated, my cheeks flushed with the highest artistic ambitions. I returned home full of a growing and almost religious veneration for art, and with my head full of Rembrandt, shut myself in the lavatory and did 'it'.*[25]

Salvador was going through puberty, a condition in which he felt very comfortable throughout his whole life. In his autobiography he liked describing over and over again how masturbation and artistic inspiration were closely related – that is, that his sexuality and his art were inseparable forms of the same ecstasy, the intoxicating sensation of being 'out-of-the-body'.

With unmistakable pride he reported in his *Secret Life* how as a youth he had continued and expanded his childish experiences and desire for 'otherness'. Doing the opposite of what others did became his motto and his teachers, in particular, reacted to it with white-hot fury. The bashful child became a shameless youth. He once told his literature teacher that his shoes saw the matter in a completely different light. His fellow-pupils were impressed and applauded his boldness, but began to wonder whether he wasn't perhaps actually mad.

The contemporary Dadaists would have adopted Dalí as one of their own. 'Anti' was their battle-cry in the struggle against any and every standpoint in political, philosophical, artistic or everyday affairs. But as Dalí as yet knew nothing about the Cabaret Voltaire in Zurich or the Armory Show in New York, his revolt had more to do with a feeling of awkwardness and a fierce urge to make a mark on the world around him.

He loved the landscape of the Empordá with all his being. *During my solitary walks the contours of the rocks and the bursts of light falling on the structure and aesthetic substance of the landscape were the unique protagonists onto whose mineral indifference I projected day by day the whole accumulated and chronically unsatisfied tension of my erotic and emotional life.*[26] His affectionate gaze was focused on what lay before his eyes and painting it could give form to his rapture.

The youthful Salvador was also aware of events going on around him. He cynically observed how during the First World War (Catalonia had sent thousands of volunteers to support France) the people of his home town had been chiefly occupied with folklore and cooking, *and I knew the whole*

DADAISM

'Dada extracted the ultimate out of the fiasco of the illusion of progress (material battles in World War One) and celebrated the triumph of the absurd, […] a desperate attempt to survive by destroying the destructive.' (*Kunst des 20. Jahrhunderts.* Cologne 2000, p 119). The phenomenon was already to be found in Paris and New York with Marcel Duchamp's 'ready-mades' and the journal *The Blind Man*), Man Ray and Francis Picabia (journal '291'), before by chance acquiring the name 'Dada'. On 5 February 1916 the artists Hugo Ball, Tristan Tzara, Richard Hülsenbeck, Hans Arp and Marcel Janko founded the Cabaret Voltaire in Zurich.

*ritual by heart: sitting outside in the sun drinking good Pernod with a piece of sugar dipped in it and listening to a string of funny stories about the nouveaux riches.*[27]

At the celebrations to mark the end of the war Dalí was to represent a group of his fellow-pupils by making the opening speech. He had intended, he said, to start by saying something like *the great sacrifice of blood made on the fields of battle has awakened with a jolt the political consciousness of all oppressed peoples.*[28] On the day, however, he lost his nerve, he was tongue-tied, felt faint and couldn't hear what was going on. When he realised that the public had come just to listen to him, he had a desire *to feel he was the object of 'total expectation'.*[29] And then it came over him, overwhelmed by the principle of opposites, that this was a gathering in support of the Allies, so he raised his arms and shouted as loud as he could: *'Long live Germany! Long live Russia!'*

*Then I flung the table violently into the auditorium [...]. Without my realising it, my action had resulted in an event of great political originality and immediacy. Martí Vilanova, one of the local agitators, explained my behaviour in his own way. 'There are now no enslaved or oppressed people any more', he said. 'Germany is in the middle of a revolution and must be met on the same footing as the victors. That applies particularly to Russia, whose social revolution is the only fruit of the war which allows us any real hope.'*[30]

It would be wrong to think of the young Dalí as a loner. He had made a lot of friends with whom he was working against the 'putrefactos', as they called members of 'rotting, decaying' society. He became a political activist, joined the anarchists and took part in a procession carrying a German flag, while Comrade Vilanova carried that of the USSR.

Spanish political life was suffering from the after-effects of the 1898 war against the USA, in which Spain had lost her colonies of Cuba, Puerto Rico and the Philippines, and this was reason enough to question the country's political relationships in general. The so-called 'ninety-eight' generation was looking for excuses for the shameful collapse of their previous worldwide empire. The major landowners, the industrial bourgeoisie and the Catholic church were the three great powers in the state and in society. The rural population and industrial workers (particularly in Catalonia) were not integrated into the political and social system but anarchists and revolutionary Marxists were claiming their rights for them.

Dalí and his friends were intent on revolution. On 12 November 1919 he wrote in his diary that he was waiting for it *with open arms and was ready for the cry of 'Long live the Soviet Republic!' And if to achieve a true democracy and a truly social republic, it is necessary to endure a tyranny first, well, long live tyranny.*[31] At school he led a protest when the school authorities were about to take action against co-education.

When the father of his friend Miravitlles, with whom he was producing the journal *Studium*, was put in prison, Salvador went to see him and was impressed by his struggle against the police. He came to the conclusion that anyone with a claim to intellectual integrity at the time would finish up in jail. He was particularly interested that the 'left' were just as concerned with politics as with liberating the arts. He and Miravitlles rented rooms at Carrer Murala 4, so that they could work undisturbed on the satirical periodical *El Sanyo Pancraci*. When this enterprise came to an end after three issues, Salvador continued to rent the rooms as a studio and completed his first murals there.

He was also acting the lover. He had a girl, Carme Roget Pumerola, whom he kissed and whose breasts he was allowed to stroke. He used all his ingenuity to get this student, whom he had met at evening classes at Art School and who was two years older than him, to fall in love with him so that he could make her suffer.

He got into trouble with Nuñez by doing the opposite of what he recommended. When he was supposed to use the lightest possible pencil strokes on the portrait of a white-haired man, he covered almost the entire canvas with black paint. Nuñez was indignant and said it would be impossible to add any white to it, whereupon Dalí took a small knife and scratched the paper very delicately until he had created the effect of the finest white hair. Nuñez was astonished and had to admire what he had done. His pupil was increasingly fighting against what was considered correct and making his own experiments; at one stage he put stones into his pictures and painted them to look like clouds.

*Everyone was saying: 'Dalí's son is now putting stones into his pictures!' but in spite of that at the height of my 'stone period' I was asked to lend some pictures to an exhibition in the hall of the Music Society. About 30 local and regional artists were exhibiting, some from Girona and even from Barcelona. My works were among those most remarked on and the two leading intellectuals of the town, Carlos Costa and Puig Pujades, declared that without the smallest doubt a brilliant career awaited me.* [32]

Salvador worked industriously, absorbed in his pictures and curious about his own potential. He was also writing poetry and even composing little treatises on the 'Great Masters of Painting'. Those on Dürer, El Greco, Goya, Leonardo, Michelangelo and Velázquez were published in the periodical *Studium*.

In a course on philosophy which he attended in the evenings, wider horizons opened up to him. He at once started writing 'The Tower of Babel'. *What was 'rational life' for everyone at the foot of the tower struck me as just death and chaos; [...] all around me I saw only compromise with this death. That was not for me; I would never make a compromise with death. My mother had died unexpectedly and that was the worst blow I had suffered in my life.*[33]

Felipa Domènech died on 6 February 1921 at the age of 47 after an operation for cancer of the uterus. *I worshipped her; to me she was unique. [...] She loved me so completely and was so proud of me that she couldn't have been wrong [...]. My mother's death struck me as an insult aimed at me by fate. [...] In tears, clenching my teeth, I swore I would tear my mother from death and fate with swords of light, which would one day bathe my famous name in their rays.*[34] Then in July 1921 his paternal friend and ally Pepito Pitxot died, too.

Everyday life in the Dalí household hardly changed with the death of Salvador's mother, because her sister, Aunt Tieta, stepped into her place and, after she had recovered from a nervous breakdown, she married his father. But for Salvador everything had changed. Up to then he had lived in a protected world. His obstinacy had flourished in the knowledge that there was always a safety net to catch him, but now his bravado was entering a new and critical phase.

Painting to defy death by creating work which could outlive him and help to win him a seat in the artists' Olympus was for the 16-year-old a general incentive which gained in intensity through his mother's early death, yet however great his rage, determination and impatience to demonstrate it to the world through his art, he knew he still had much to learn.

In Catalan the word 'Dalí' means 'desire'

Though the positive opinions of Pepito Pitxot, Carlos Costa and Puig Pujades had not yet convinced Salvador's father of his son's artistic potential, he was apparently finally persuaded by the highly flattering review of eight of Salvador's paintings on exhibit in the Galeria Dalmau, which appeared on the front page of *La Tribuna,* the Barcelona daily newspaper. They were outstanding among the 140 paintings by art students. Josep Dalmau, Barcelona art dealer and gallery-owner, specialised in the moderns and was a pioneer in Spain with his exhibitions of the impressionists, fauvists and cubists, including Matisse, Picasso, Gris, Picabia and Miró.

Don Salvador Dalí y Cusí took Salvador to Madrid where he wanted to study painting, his only condition being that his son should aim for a university degree, which would qualify him to become a professor.

# A holy trickster: how to study art (1922-1928)

Dalí wanted to study at the venerable San Fernando Royal Academy of Fine Arts, founded in 1742 by the Bourbon King Philip V. The entrance exam consisted in making a scale copy of a plaster cast of Jacopo Sansovino's *Bacchus*. Dalí's effort was much smaller than specified but so perfect that it was accepted. His father and sister went home very relieved.

On 30 September 1922 at the age of 18, he enrolled in the faculties of perspective, anatomy, history of art (ancient and medieval) and plastic drawing. On Sundays he studied alone in the Prado, where with his own eyes he could feast upon the originals of the little reproductions in his books: works by Hieronymus Bosch, Diego Velázquez, Francisco Goya, El Greco, José Ribera – all great names in the history of art.

His mother's brother Anselm Domènech, who owned a bookshop in Barcelona, provided him with books and magazines which led him beyond impressionism into the modern world. He also ordered the French Communist newspaper *L'Humanité* and the Parisian art journal *L'Esprit Nouveau* and was eager to catch up with the moderns. Having just discovered cubism for himself, he created in the Prado his *sketches of various paintings composed in cubist style*.[35] At the end of the 19th century the impressionists – and also Cézanne – had drawn new conclusions from the view that representing a supposedly objective reality could not do justice to the 'real' relationship of people to things. To interpret reality as a collection of discrete physical objects to be weighed and measured and presented as solid bodies meant blindly following the pre-judgment of mechanical physics. Drawing on late 19th-century psychology, these artists were fascinated with the process of perception. If human beings' association with and grasp of reality was to be the starting point for painting, it became clear that objects only materialised in the barely detectable transitional process of perception. Thus the actual world does not appear as a finished product before one's eyes but is built up by one's senses. Objects, then, would simply be transitional products within this process, through which human senses would create their perceived world.

Cézanne explored this by lightly breaking up colour relationships, and by fracturing them into a myriad gradations attempted to reproduce his experience of what resists representation. With his principle of the 'passage' he focused on the perceptual experience of things in continuous flux or process. He is regarded as an originator of today's 'classical' modernists, because his paintings emphasise perspective, construction and abstraction. Contemporaries found this disturbing but the modernists developed further along these same lines.

Cubism, which began with Picasso's *Demoiselles d'Avignon* (1907), carried this fracturing to its ultimate conclusion. All works of art are based on balls, cones and cubes (circles, triangles and rectangles), which appear as the raw material from which everything else is derived and thereby produce basic forms and patterns and ways of arranging them – hardly noticeable to a normal glance but highly effective (and virtually involuntarily so). There is something analogous in Nietzsche's psychology: his disclosure of the secret workings of mental associations has profoundly influenced modern psychology and is reflected both in the depth-psychology schools of Sigmund Freud, Carl Gustav Jung and Alfred Adler and in the paintings of Giorgio de Chirico.

Dalí's compatriot Pablo Picasso was 23 years his senior. He set up his first studio in Barcelona and after his so-called pink and blue periods experimented with different perspectives in the same work. What Cézanne saw as transition, the cubists turned into an integrated, virtually simultaneous whole. Unlike him, they loved big-city life and put collages into their pictures made up of man-made objects from the everyday urban scene. To them daily life and art were no longer separate, opposite spheres but were integrated by means of fracturing images. Cubist pictures presented an inventory of café life: absinthe bottles, pipes, glasses, jugs, newspapers and guitars.

Another stream of modernism was on the move in Italy, where the futurists were impressed by the dynamism of city life, in which even the physical world did not stand still and everything was striving towards the future. Kandinsky came to the conclusion that in art everything was permissible. Society was no longer formed and upheld by the stable principles of God, king, fatherland, reason and morals which had formerly ruled over everyday life.

This attitude was elevated by the dadaists to the level of a principle – with sensational effect. Collage was an ideal medium to demonstrate that fracturing is associated with fragmentation but this is no longer expressed in aesthetic sublimation but by introducing prefabricated, 'ready-made' matter, which became just as much the artists' raw material as clay or paint. From 1919 on Max Ernst was using an indirect method of collage, by taking apart woodcuts, among other things, and reassembling them to create his pictorial 'novels'. Marcel Duchamp went a step further when he took everyday objects with no innate artistic attributes and declared them to be art. If art were not to be confined to the function of mirroring the outer world but relocated to the production site of the onlooker's own perceptions, even a mundane object removed from the normal context of its function would reveal its hitherto undetected artistic content. Only when an artefact collided with art in the catalyst of an exhibition would

Dalí with his close friend Federico García Lorca

the former take on the character of an artwork. It merely needed to be displaced and authenticated with a signature.

As for Dalí, his next move was to focus on the paintings of the Spaniard Juan Gris, who had developed synthetic cubism in 1910, and he imitated him by painting almost entirely in monochrome. *As a reaction against my earlier colouristic and impressionistic phases the only colours on my palette were white, black, sienna and olive green.*[36] In the journal *Valori plastici* he had come across the paintings of Giorgio de Chirico and his essays on metaphysical painting.

At first he avoided his fellow-students, shut himself in his room as though in a hermit's cell and there he painted, but to show everyone that he was now a real artist he acquired a large, black felt hat and a pipe, which he didn't actually smoke but always had hanging from the corner of his mouth, wore velvet jackets, flowing cravats and a long cloak and sported shoulder-length hair and a cane with a gilded knob.

When he left the provinces in 1922 Salvador's youthful revolt against the 'putrefactos', as he called the petite-bourgeoisie of Figueres, grew into a liberation movement of unforeseen scope. He lived in the Residencia de Estudiantes, a modern hostel housing about 150 students, independent of any church or state influence. Buñuel wrote in *My Last Sigh*: 'The residencia, privately funded, was a sort of campus in English university style and a single room only cost seven pesetas a day. It was run by Don Alberto Jimenez, a very cultivated man from Malaga. You could follow any conceivable course of study; there were lecture rooms, five laboratories, a library and several sports grounds. You could stay there as long as you liked.'[37]

The natural enemies of the young were the art professors, who represented a Spain which held aloof from current European cultural developments. Dalí was indignant that they offered him nothing relevant to the craft of painting. He was told to give expression to his mood when he painted, which was nothing new to him. Before he left Figueres he had already noted: *I believe that one has to paint for the sake of painting without any aesthetic doctrine, accept no restrictions and follow the impulses of one's completely emancipated sensibility [...].*[38]

But there were technical questions. *I wanted to learn how to mix and apply paints, how to match them to each other, how best to prepare a canvas and how to absorb all the technical knowledge to be gained from the great masters. In fact my teachers knew nothing of the real essentials. [...] Only one found favour in my eyes – José Moreno Carbonero, one of the oldest, an assured master of his craft which he pursued with impeccable conscientiousness.*[39]

Fellow-protesters like José (Pepin) Bello and Cristino Mallo remembered Dalí as being extremely shy and modest at first. He did in fact particularly feel his inadequacy when he got to know the Andalusian poet Federico García Lorca, who had lived in the residencia since 1919. Lorca became his revered model, rival

FEDERICO GARCÍA LORCA
(1898-1936)

'Spanish poet of the younger generation, reviver of Spanish romances and ballad plays and master of poetic imagery' (Hermann Pongs). From 1919 he lived in the Residencia de Estudiantes in Madrid, where he met Buñuel and Dalí. He was shot by the Falangists in the Spanish Civil War. Poetry: *Collected Poems* (1921), *Songs* (1927), *Gypsy Ballads* (1928), *Poetry of the Cante Jondo* (1931). Dramatic poems: *Mariana Pineda* (1925), *The Prodigious Cobbler's Wife* (1930), *Blood Wedding* (1933), *The House of Bernarda Alba* (1936).

and closest friend and for a while they shared a room.

*In the hostel intellectual snobbery had led to cliques being formed and a small group of avant-garde writers and painters had gathered around Federico García Lorca, Luis Buñuel and Eugenio Montes. One of them, Pepin Bello, passed the open door of my room one day and saw a cubist painting on my easel. He told the others of his astonishment and they, having thought me a reactionary, were agreeably surprised at my avant-gardism. [...] They welcomed me as one of themselves.*[40]

Luis Buñuel, a reluctant student of agriculture, natural sciences, philosophy and literature and national boxing champion in 1921, had long been searching for his real métier. Four years older than Dalí, he had been at Madrid University since 1917 and knew his way around the city's nightlife. *In the Crystal Palace, one of the most elegant Madrid tea-rooms, I had my baptism of fire. When we made our entrance – I went in first in my anarchist artist's uniform – it had a sensational effect [...].*[41]

By talking all night about God and the world, the relationship between provincial life and life in Madrid, Spain and Europe and Spanish society's need for rejuvenation, about poetry, painting and philosophy, Lorca, Dalí and Buñuel found they had become a close-knit trio. Last but not least, they shared an interest in psycho-

LUIS BUÑUEL (1900-1983)

Spanish film-maker (Oscar winner, 1972) who had to flee Spain after the Civil War (1936-1939) because of his left-wing activities. After the surrealist experimental films he made with Dalí - *Un Chien Andalou* (1928) and *L'Age d'Or* (1930) – and a film of social criticism *Las Hurdes* (1932), he made a number of films in Mexico. He won international recognition with *Viridiana* (1961), *The Exterminating Angel* (1962), *Diary of a Chambermaid* (1964), *Belle de Jour* (1967), *Tristana* (1970), *The Discreet Charm of the Bourgeoisie* (1972), *The Phantom of Liberty* (1974) and *That Obscure Object of Desire* (1977). The main themes of all his films are the ambivalence and paradox of the world of bourgeois, religious and sexual life with all its rituals.

analysis. In 1922 the Biblioteca Nueva published a Spanish translation of Sigmund Freud's 'Collected Works' and Dalí was later to declare that psychoanalysis was one of the pivotal discoveries of his life.

All three admired the French poets Apollinaire, Pierre Réverdy and Jean Cocteau, the painters Pablo Picasso and Juan Gris, the Russian stage designer Sergei Diaghilev, the Italian futurist Marinetti and the Chilean poet Vicente Huidobro. Paris was then the hub of the avant garde and became their lodestar; everything of significance was happening there and to Paris they must go.

Among Spanish artists they thought highly of Ortega y Gasset, Unamuno, Valle-Inclan and d'Ors and especially the poets Moreno Vila and Ramón

Dalí with Luis Buñuel

Gómez de la Serna. The last-named particularly interested them, because during the First World War he had met the dadaists in Switzerland and France and knew Tristan Tzara and Picasso personally. Like Francis Picabia, de la Serna had a penchant for juxtaposing vivid images from apparently unrelated spheres of reality. They considered that analogies between the soul within a natural object and its outward appearance were suitable tools for promoting the dadaists' abolition of logic in order to set free unconscious associations. De la Serna called his poems 'greguerias', or gibberish ('literally, pigs squeaking'). They are vignettes which open up a wide range of meaning – they alienate and are deliberately anti-reasonable and anti-classical. For instance: 'The moon moves faster and climbs higher when dogs bay at it' or: 'screws are nails with their hair parted in the middle.'[42]

In the group gathered round de la Serna in the Café Pombo, the talk was all about the newest publications, poems, politics, foreign journals and foreign books and in the residencia they organised lectures with discussions, to bring these themes to the notice of the other students.

Avid to make an impression, Dalí continued in this new sphere of activities the wilful, distorted self-dramatisation of his childhood. Both among his friends and in the Academia he behaved like the 'holy trickster' of Indian mythology. The depth psychologist C G Jung saw 'typical motifs of a trickster' when the hero liked playing cunning tricks (partly in jest, partly malicious-ly), could transmogrify, had a split personality (half beast, half god), surrendered to any kind of torment and – not least – resem-bled a bringer of healing – 'Salvador', the saviour.[43]

Salvador took his name seriously and saw himself – not just in jest – as the 'saviour' of modern painting. He was convinced of his mission and his serious ambition was in no way lessened by the fact that he was playing a part. He could talk about his mega-lomania, narcissism and exhibitionism with ironic detachment and deliberately orchestrated his entrances like an actor stepping onto the stage. Continually doing the opposite of what was socially accepted as the norm caught on among his fellow-students, who called it 'being dalish'. At the same time his obses-sion with painting made him a model student, industrious, enquiring and eager to explore the scope of his own potential. If he felt that a professor, a traditionally minded custodian of art, had nothing to offer him, he became arrogant and aggressive, yet he did not wait for anyone else to help him and followed his own urge towards perfection. He told his colleagues: *If you refuse to study draughtsmanship, perspective, anatomy, aesthetic mathematics and the theory of colours, I tell you that I regard that as a sign of laziness rather than of genius.*[44]

He spent the summer vacation of 1923 painting once again in his studio in Cadaqués – portraits of his sister Ana Maria, landscapes of the Empordá with figures, Cadaqués viewed from the tower on Cape Creus and gypsies from Figueres – and experimented with cubist constructions (*All Forms derive from the Square; Harlequin, sitting at a Table*), still-life compositions and self-portraits. On his return to university in the autumn he enrolled in courses on preparing canvases, history of art (modern and present-day), copperplate engraving and still-life drawing.

On 17 October 1923 the appointments board held a public election for an academic chair and when only two professors voted for Daniel Vazquez Diaz, the students' choice, they rioted and the police were called in. Dalí was questioned by the Rector, Miguel Blay, and protested his innocence, but in vain. When he refused to divulge the names of those responsible, he was suspended for a year and also barred from sitting the examinations. This may have served to enhance his prestige but it was also extremely embarrassing. Though he had difficulty in making his father understand the situation, he did eventually succeed in winning his support.

POLITICAL DEVELOPMENTS

In 1909, sparked by economic and social conditions, there was an uprising in Catalonia against the central government and the church. In order to prevent a similar movement after the First World War (in which Spain remained neutral), King Alfonso XIII introduced in 1923 a military dictatorship under Primo de Rivera. In 1931 it – and with it the monarchy – came to an end when the left-wing parties won the elections, which they did again in 1936. Thereupon General Franco started a revolt against the left which led to the Spanish Civil War.

Señor Dalí came to Madrid, argued vehemently with the Rector and produced legal arguments to support his case, but to no avail. The Rector told him that Salvador was a bolshevik in his painting and when he appealed to the Education Ministry he met with no more success. However, it is possible that while independently searching out and developing his artistic visions in his studio, Salvador was learning more than he would have at the Academy.

In Figueres he was involved in a sensational event. On the occasion of a surprise visit to the town by King Alfonso XIII potential troublemakers, including Dalí, his political colleague Martí Vilanova and the militant Communist Jaume Miravitlles, were taken into custody. On 21 May Dalí was put in solitary confinement in Figueres, nine days later transferred to the prison in Girona and on 11 June released by the military judge without charge. It was generally assumed that this action was aimed at Dalí's father as a warning, because after Primo de Rivera's coup d'état he had petitioned against electoral fraud on the part of the right wing. Shortly before his son's arrest the Guardia Civil searched his house but found no incriminating material.[45]

On his return from prison, Dalí received a hero's welcome in Figueres. He later wrote: *In theory I belonged to the far left and sympathised with the Communists and Anarchists. I wore overalls, subscribed to* L'Humanité *and raged against the bourgeoisie of Figueres. […] We were a band of revolutionaries. […] One of the militia even gave the order to shave my head.* [46]

Like every painter, even Dalí was bound to absorb the artistic viewpoints of his contemporaries, however headstrong and exaggeratedly ambitious he was to be. Contrary to his own account, Spanish painters like Joaquin Mir, Joaquin Sunyer, Maria Blanchard and Rafael Barradas had already been experimenting with the potential of cubist forms before he did. Landscapes, people and things were being deconstructed, and then reconstructed according to the principles of geometric figuration.

One striking example is a painting of Dalí's called *Cubist Self-portrait* (1923; 104.9 x 74.2 cm), a gouache with collage on cardboard. The surface gives the impression of a pleated skirt cut into strips, which are broken up diagonally into countless tiny areas of rhythmically varied blue. Light ochre-coloured newspaper cuttings with capital letters are placed at an angle in the blue patches and clay pipes lying on them complete the kaleidoscope of colours. In the top third of the surface, slightly to the left of centre and also ochre-coloured, the outline of a face has been inserted with accentuated arched eyebrows and a dark semi-circle to indicate the hair. The picture looks like the determined statement of a student: 'I have got it, I can do cubism!' or 'I am deep into cubism!'

His father was proud of his son's work. When Salvador asked his former drawing teacher Juan Nuñez to show him how to make copperplate engravings, his father immediately bought a press and installed it in the house. In 1925 he bought a large scrapbook in which he collected newspaper cuttings, announcements of exhibitions, photographs and anything else about his son's artistic and political development. Though Salvador's commercial success while still a student exceeded his father's expectations, he feared that this might make him lose the motivation to become a professor of art.

But the solicitous father knew that his son felt 'simply a vocation to paint', [47] without having any idea of his true motivation, which

SALVADOR DALÍ Y DOMÈNECH THROUGH HIS FATHER'S EYES
After 21 years of great care and effort I finally saw my son in a position to make his own way in the world. [...] We, his parents, were not in favour of his dedicating himself wholly to art, for which he had felt a vocation since he was a child. I still believe that art is not a suitable means of earning one's living. It is simply and solely an intellectual relaxation to be enjoyed in one's leisure time. [...] However, [...] I do not believe that I have the right to oppose such a determined vocation, seeing that another, very decisive handicap exists, which is his 'intellectual laziness' in all fields.

was a violent fear and hatred of mediocrity above anything else. He protested against the traditional life-style of the older generation in the typical manner of young people of his age, but unlike most of them he felt he had a vocation to recreate his own life along new lines. He had chosen art in order to rescue and carry over into adulthood a child's life-style, free of the constraints of bourgeois conformity and cares about financial security. Only in art could he make the principle of being different, eccentric and contrary the principal ingredient in moulding his life-style.

*When I had finished 'doing time', I went back to Madrid where my friends were waiting for me with feverish impatience, admitting that without me 'the world looked different'. […] I was greeted with applause, coddled and pampered. I had become their god. They did everything for me, […] rushing out like knights errant to conquer the dragons of orthodoxy which stood in the way of my putting my wildest fantasies into effect.* [48]

Dalí looked on jealously as Lorca shone and impressed the others in the readings at the 'residencia' and also in the café where they held their *literary meetings.*[49] *Maldoror was overshadowing my life and just then there came another shadow - that of Federico García Lorca. For a while an eclipse darkened the virginal whiteness of my spirit and my senses.* [50] *The Songs of Maldoror* was an extraordinary set of poems by one Isidore Ducasse (1846-1870) who, under the assumed name of Comte de Lautréamont, only became famous 50 years after his early death, when the songs were discovered by the surrealist André Breton, who printed them in 1919 in the *Journal Littérature.*[51] The Spanish translation which now came out in the *Biblioteca Nueva* fascinated everyone.

These verses were variously dubbed 'Poetry of transgression' (Gilbert Lascault), 'Romanticism of revolt' (Leon Pierre Quint) and 'Poetry of evil' (Klaus Bittermann). The most quoted passage is Lautréamont's affectionate description of the beauty of a boy, which he compares to the 'chance meeting of a sewing machine and an umbrella on a dissecting table'. [52] There was hardly a single surrealist painter who did not illustrate the 'Songs' and Dalí added his contribution in 1934. These verses made history; now absolutely everything had become possible in poetry, as in art.

In the sixth poem Lautréamont wrote: 'But should one be ashamed of intimacy in the case of a strong and passionate friendship of serious, confident devotion?' [53] Dalí was already in love with Lorca's poetry and Lorca loved Dalí's paintings. Lorca was homosexual, as Dalí knew; was everything then possible in life as well? In any case the painter invited the poet to spend the 1925 Easter holidays with his family at their house in Cadaqués.

Lorca presented Dalí's father with a personally dedicated copy of his recently published *Canciones (Songs)* and both Señor Dalí and the 17-year-old Ana Maria were impressed with him. They took him immediately to their hearts, considered him the greatest Spanish poet of the future and invited guests to hear him read from his drama *Mariana Pineda*, for a Barcelona stage production of which Dalí helped Lorca design the sets. The two students enjoyed life on the beach in the spring sunshine and Dalí showed his friend all the places he had loved since his childhood and felt free from the need to outshine everybody. Lorca undoubtedly loved him. Ana Maria was captivated by her brother's talented friend who was very kind to her, too, and she knew nothing of his feelings towards Salvador.

Later Dalí said that *people tended to denigrate my relationship with Lorca (which the poet himself acknowledged), as though it was a sugary kitsch romance, whereas it was actually the exact opposite: it was an erotic and tragic love – tragic, because it could not be reciprocal.* [54]

Lorca sublimated his relationship with his friend and the world of Cadaqués in 'Ode to Salvador Dalí', published in the April 1926 edition of José Ortega y Gasset's periodical *Revista de Occidente*. Dalí's biographer Ian Gibson reported: 'It was presumably in May of that year (1926) that García Lorca tried to seduce Dalí […]. In 1955 Dalí told Alain Bosquet that the poet had twice tried to sodomise him but that nothing had happened […].' Dalí remembered: *Not having succeeded in persuading me to put my arm at his disposal, he swore to me that the sacrifice exacted from the girl was as great as his own: it was the first time he had had intercourse with a woman.* [55] The poet had insisted on Dalí at least watching what happened. [56]

Dalí's letters to Lorca were full of endearments; he called him *dear Lorca, dear son* or *fat little Japanese* when he was particularly enthusiastic about his poetry. He also occasionally signed himself *your little son.* [57] For his part, Lorca not only loved and praised Dalí but was studying his friend's psychology very closely. He saw a kind of formal compulsion at work in the pattern of Dalí's life and art. 'Dalí won't let himself go. He needs to be in control […]' [58]

Tomfoolery and extravaganza, impudence, arrogance, theatrical entrances and general craziness were Salvador's ways of establishing a compromise between the elemental, seductive urge to continue his childish, mudpie-making identification with the earth and the crystalline calculation of detached superiority. The reversible figures and double images in his paintings can be similarly interpreted as attempts to reconcile precision with chaos in the dichotomy of human life. Dalí's interest lay in uniting image and counter-image in a single paradox, as though he wanted to demonstrate that you can portray things as accurately as you want in words or paint, but that they will still have no clear meaning – only the fluctuating impact of insoluble enigmas.

Dalí's vision was to put into paint or writing this fundamental experience, which can both offend and fascinate. Formal compulsion to perfect one's craft and technique and the continual elusiveness of a clear meaning are two sides of the same coin. Later he put this into words: *When I paint and I myself don't understand what I am painting, that certainly does not mean that my images have no meaning [...].*[59]

Lorca and Dalí missed the visit to the residencia of the French surrealist Louis Aragon on 18 April 1925. Aragon made a speech announcing the birth of a new spirit of rebellion and an attack on everything traditional – in short, the advent of surrealism. A report

GARCÍA LORCA'S
'ODE TO
SALVADOR DALÍ'
(1926)

O Salvador Dalí, of the olive-coloured voice!
I do not praise your halting , youthful brush
or your pigments that flirt with the pigment of your times,
but I extol your longing for eternity with boundaries. [...]
Vanquished death takes refuge, trembling,
in the tight circle of the present moment. [...]
You, a painter, refuse to let your forms be softened
by the shifting cotton of an unexpected cloud. [...]
You love a matter definite and exact,
where fungus cannot take hold.
You love architecture which builds on the absent
and admit the flag simply as a jest. [...]
I sing your restless longing for the statue,
your fear of the emotions that await you in the street. [...]
But above all I sing the common thought
That unites us in dark and golden hours.
The light that dazzles our eyes is not art.
Rather it is love, friendship and crossing swords.

appeared in the June edition of the journal *La Révolution Surréaliste*, which Dalí could certainly have seen in the residencia.

Dalí was now only attending the Academia for short periods between painting and submitting his works to exhibitions. At the Palacio de Velazquez in Madrid's Retiro Park on 27 May 1925 the Spanish Minister of Culture Eduardo Marquina opened an exhibition of the newly founded 'Sociedad Iberica Artistas', which was intended to be a forum for modern art in the capital. Dalí was thought to have written a flyer attacking the Academia and defending 'the painters of our time', such as 'Derain, Picasso, Matisse, Braque, Juan Gris, Severini, Picabia and de Chirico'. In the exhibition were eleven of his pictures, among them a portrait of his friend Luis Buñuel, who remembered it as '… a very exact portrait, for which he had divided the whole canvas into small squares and copied the measurements of my nose and my lips completely accurately.'[60]

'The show launched Dalí triumphantly in Madrid.'[61] His works, which stood out from those by 39 other Spanish artists in the exhibition, were praised not only by the art critic José Moreno Villa, who knew him from the residencia, but also by Eugeni d'Ors – 'probably the most celebrated authority on art in the country' [62] – and the hispanist Jean Cassou in the *Mercure de France*.

Taking and passing the end-of-term examination seemed just a minor detail to Dalí and in September his father informed the Academia that his son would not be returning in the autumn of 1925/26 but would prepare privately for his examinations and register again for them in the spring of 1926.

During the summer of 1925 Dalí was painting from dawn to dusk for his first solo exhibition from 14 to 27 November at the Galería Dalmau in Barcelona. This comprised 22 works (17 paintings and five drawings), 18 of which he had produced in the course of the year and eight of which were portraits of Ana Maria.

Reviews and sales exceeded all expectations and on 21 November Dalmau honoured his 21-year old protégé with a formal banquet in the Hotel España in Barcelona, followed by another on 5 December in Figueres. Dalí wrote to Lorca about his success and told him enthusiastically about the beautiful postcards from Buñuel and from their friends José Maria Hinojosa and Juan Vicens in Paris, asking him to visit them there soon.

On 11 April 1926, chaperoned by his sister and stepmother, Dalí travelled to the Mecca of modern art and life, where Buñuel took his provincial Spanish guests under his wing. Highlights included visiting the Louvre, Picasso, Spanish friends and, on the return journey through Brussels, seeing Vermeer's paintings. When he called on Picasso in the Rue de la Boetie, he took with him his picture *Girl of Figueres,* which Picasso apparently looked at carefully. His comments were encouraging and he spent two hours showing his visitor his own recent paintings in so-called classical style.

In contrast to this experience, the Academia seemed to Dalí increasingly like a handicap and he dealt quickly in his own way with the examinations on 14 June, by refusing to sit them. According to the minutes drawn up immediately afterwards, he said: *'No! Since all the teachers at the San Fernando School are incompetent to judge me, I'm withdrawing.'* The board, understandably, was outraged. [63]

Dalí was once again expelled from the Academia, this time permanently, by a royal decree of 20 October 1926. He simply walked out, without even taking his personal possessions with him. These were his later comments on this behaviour: *The motives for my action were simple: I wanted to have done with the School of Fine Art and with the orgiastic life of Madrid once and for all; I wanted to be forced to escape all that and come back to Figueres to work for a year, after which I would try to convince my father that my studies should continue in Paris. Once there, with the work that I would bring with me, I would definitely seize power!* [64] His father was horrified but could do nothing about it in retrospect.

Dalí came into his own in Port Lligat on the coast of Cape Creus and told Lorca that he had recovered his equilibrium. *All the cliffs and ledges of Cape Creus are in a ceaseless state of metamorphosis. They variously suggest to the imagination an eagle, a camel, a cock, a lion or a woman… If one approaches the Cape from the sea, the symbolism unfolds and changes as the distance lessens. The bird becomes a bird of prey, then a piece of poultry. […] As soon as we land, however, the granite under our feet, having kept making fools of us, suddenly becomes hard, compact, smooth and implacable. My thoughts are like that […]. I am convinced that I myself am Cape Creus – that I am the incarnation of the living heart of this landscape […], that I keep metamorphosing into a semblance of Cape Creus.* [65]

The paintings Dalí made between 1925 and 1928 vary in tendency and clearly show the influences of Giorgio de Chirico's 'metaphysical' painting and Picasso's massively physical sculptural works from the early 1920s, particularly in the various versions of *Venus and a Sailor* (1925) and the monumental figures in *Figure on the Rocks (Femme Couchée)* and *Sleeping Women on the Shore* (both 1926). Beside them stand works which proclaimed that he was emulating the hyper-realist still-life paintings of the 16th and 17th century Dutch masters. In 1953 he spoke of *edible beauty.* [66] Paintings like *Young Girl from Behind* and *Basket of Bread* or the drawing *Female Nude*, all from 1926, were executed with pedantic realism. He admitted freely that he loved precise drawing in the style of Ingres, whom he quoted in the catalogue of his first one-man show: 'Drawing is integrity in art'. Some of his paintings were reminiscent of the Italian Mario Sironi, particularly *Portrait of my Father, Young Girl with Bare Back* and *Young*

Portrait of Paul Éluard, 1929 (oil on board).
Private collection

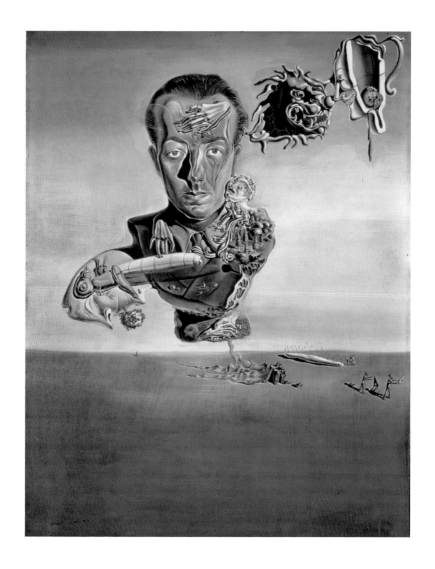

*Girl leaning on her Elbows or Ana Maria Dalí, the Painter's Sister,* all executed in 1925.

One can also detect resonances from the early surrealist works of André Masson, Yves Tanguy and Joan Miró. In particular, the drawing which served as a sketch for his first surrealist painting – *Honey is Sweeter than Blood* (1927) – reminds one of Masson's *'Dessins Automatiques'*. Most of these works were painted after his sensational exit from the Academia.

In 1927 and 1928 he was not only producing pictures but a series of articles on art, in which he was beginning to define his position as a surrealist. He wrote not only about painting but also about the art of photography and about both art and anti-art films. Some of these articles appeared in the Catalan journal *L'Amic de les Arts* and some in the international *Gaceta Literaria*, which also published film reviews from Paris by Luis Buñuel and articles by Lorca, Sebastià Gasch, Lluis Montanyà and other friends of Dalí's. He was also experimenting with surrealism in poetry. We gain a special insight into his own views on art in this period through his assessment of the style of Joan Miró, who ranked Dalí's pictures so highly that he sent his Paris dealer Pierre Loeb to see him.

> *Joan Miró's pictures lead us along a path of automatism and surreality to the point when we can nearly recognise and appraise reality itself. This proves that André Breton was right when he said that surreality is contained in reality and vice versa. Through the passive state of automatism [...] Joan Miró produces a reciprocal effect between surreality and reality with limitless possibilities for creating enigmas [...].* [67]

Giving visible form to the enigmatic became Dalí's main objective – a sort of artistic credo – and ways and means to do this were only open to the avant garde, since art forms are linked to their times. In fact, Dalí believed that there was an avant-garde component in historical works of art, when he looked at the purposes of the emerging medium of photography: *Vermeer van Delft was different. In all the history of sight his eyes were an example of the utmost probity, even when tempted by seductive tricks of light. Vermeer [...] preserved the integrity of his subjects with a totally photographic inspiration which sprang from his self-effacing but passionate tactile sense. Knowing how to see is a completely new system of surveying the scene intellectually. Knowing how to see is a way of inventing and no invention was ever as pure as that which created an aesthetically neutral view through Zeiss's glass-clear lash-less eye. [...] A photographic lens can caress the cool softness of a white wash-basin; it can follow the sleepy languor of an aquarium [...].* [68]

Dalí was obsessed by the paradox that the intangible was visible. Many years later he put this into words: *Painting is a hand-made colour photograph of virtual, over-refined, exaggerated and hyper-aesthetic images of things which are concrete but irrational.* [69]

# The riddle of the sur-real: unknown horizons of reality (1929-1939)

In April 1929 Dalí went to Paris for the second time. 'In those days Paris was the unchallenged metropolis of the art world. 45,000 painters, it was said, lived in the city [...].' [70] Joan Miró introduced Dalí to the circle of the surrealists. For Dalí surrealism meant *a revolution in life and morals,*[71] which would abolish the single dimension in human beings at a time when western society and culture were subjecting them to practicality and necessity and thus narrowly circumscribing the scope for giving free rein to their spirituality. Establishment art and the traditions of religion, morals and reason protected society and culture from the invasion of individuality. The surrealist revolution therefore strove to mobilise those spiritual forces at work unnoticed beyond and above ('sur') the ingrained patterns of experience and behaviour, known as 'the done thing'.

For the surrealists intangible dream images were the prime phenomena with which they endeavoured to enliven the spiritually excluded in western civilisation, by offering them an art designed to upset them. In dream-reality, which involuntarily determines a major part of human conscious thought, there are spiritual connections to which the laws of space, time, historicity and logic do not apply. Even when we are asleep the life of the soul is not resting; it is simply moving according to different terms of reference: vivid imagery, condensation, displacement, sub-stitution, reversal and abolition of the theory of contradiction – to mention just a few features of Sigmund Freud's theory of dreams.

The Surrealist Group, c.1920: (from left to right)
Tristan Tzara (1896-1963), Paul Éluard (1895-1952),
André Breton (1896-1966), Hans Arp (1886-1966), Dalí,
Yves Tanguy (1900-55), Max Ernst (1891-1976), René Crevel (1900-35)
and Man Ray (1890-1976)

In 1922 the group started publishing 'dream texts' as an art form in the journal *Littérature* (founded in 1919 by Breton, Soupault and Aragon). They did not want to explain or give a retrospective narrative context to the pictorial, the intangible, the absurd or the paradoxical, the full explosive might of which should be unleashed in a powerful onslaught on the reader. The historical context in which this respect for the elemental could best be appreciated, according to Philippe Soupault,[72] was the general climate of war-torn Europe in 1918. 'War … brainwashing … books about home … old soldiers … father victory … the amputees … the gassed … the shell-shocked […]. Night had fallen. André Breton and I only escaped from its darkness thanks to our dreams.'[73]

From the beginning the surrealist movement had also had its

political side. Communism seemed to some, like Aragon and Crevel, to guarantee the realisation of a new image of man. The godfather of surrealism was the poet and art critic Apollinaire and by 1929 it had already acquired a highly dramatic history of its own and a large number of followers whose works had become famous. Among the earliest of these were the painters Max Ernst, Hans Arp, Joan Miró, René Magritte, Yves Tanguy and Francis Picabia – and also Man Ray and André Masson.

Salvador Dalí was looking for comrades-in-arms. In 1928 his painting *Dialogue on the Beach (Unsatisfied Desires)* was rejected by the Autumn Salon in Barcelona as scandalous and incomprehensible. He reacted in a public lecture with a philippic against *Catalan art today in relation to the most recent expressions of youthful intelligence.* [74] 'Putrid' art would have to defend itself against the uncharted ways of the spirit and surreality!

Dalí had left cubist experimentation behind him. In *Dialogue on the Beach* he was following in the footsteps of Miró and Tanguy. On a flat, bright, ochre-coloured surface he placed organic forms, such as the pale cream and pinkish piece of flotsam, reminiscent of Hans Arp's body sculptures, which lies at a slant in the right foreground on a patch of dark, coarse-grained sand and shells on a beach stretching to the horizon.

On a curved protuberance is a rounded minimalist mouth, from which a small, thin, red flag emerges like a tongue. A fleeting, sketchy, mirage-like organic

It cannot be denied that the poetic, visionary content of these pictures is extraordinarily dense and explosively powerful. In any case nothing since the works Max Ernst produced between 1923 and 1924 [...], or Miró in 1924, [...] has taken on such a 'revelatory' character. Nothing is better accomplished or more consistently developed than the 'paranoiac-critical activity' which Dalí claimed exclusively for himself and which he defined most aptly as 'a spontaneous method of irrational recognition, based on the critical and systematic objectivisation of illusory associations and interpretations.

(André Breton, *Entretiens (Conversations)*

shape, delicately outlined with a thin, dark line and ending in a pointing finger (above it again is something like a tiny red flag) rises diagonally into the bright blue of the sky. On the left of the shore a deformed, solid, pale pink hand rests on a smaller rectangle of dark sand, holding between two of its fingers a mouth or female genitals and another finger is pointing. Flat and lineal, fleeting and tangible, rising and reposing – everything is harmonised in a formally beautiful composition. Though the deformed hand is isolated, it does not seem to have been cut off. Everything floats between form and abstraction and the viewer's gaze can wander and linger at will.

It is hard to believe that this picture was interpreted as unequivocally demonstrating that in real life the painter could not deal with the intimate orifice in a woman's body. Dalí's paintings tend to function as tests for his interpreters. We learn a lot about touchy sexual and moral issues, vulgar psychology and the psychosexual problems of those who, while virtually shouting 'stop, thief', profess to be writing about art. However, reducing a work of art to a mere symptom of the personal psychic state of the artist will teach one little about it.

Together with Luis Buñuel, whose mother gave him the money to make a film, Dalí wrote a screenplay designed to express in artistic terms the surrealist world of antithesis. Buñuel described how they did it. 'We accepted the first images that occurred to us, systematically rejecting those deriving from culture or education. They had to be images which surprised us and which we both accepted without discussion. Only that. For example: the woman grasps a tennis racquet to protect herself from the man who wants to attack her. Then he looks around for something with which to counterattack and (now I'm talking to Dalí): "What does he see?" "A flying toad." "Bad!" "A bottle of brandy." "Bad!" "Well then, two ropes." "Good, but after the ropes?" "He pulls them and falls, because they're tied to something very heavy." "Ah, then it's good for him to fall." "With the ropes come two big gourds." "What else?" "Two Marist Brothers." "That's it, two Marist Brothers." "Next?" "A cannon." "Bad." "A luxurious armchair." "No, a grand piano." "Terrific, and on top of it a donkey ... no, two rotting donkeys. Fantastic!" That's to say, we encouraged irrational images to erupt unexplained.'[75]

This was in line with surrealist method. Dalí and Buñuel were discovering that film could be dream language. When after long deliberation they thought of the title *Un Chien Andalou* they laughed themselves sick, because nowhere in the film was there

Portrait of Luis Buñuel, 1924 (oil on canvas). Museo Nacional Centro de Arte Reina Sofia, Madrid, Spain

an Andalusian dog. The film was shot in Paris and Buñuel asked Dalí to collect a few ants just before setting off from Cadaqués and to transport them carefully to Paris, because he could not get hold of any there. They were to crawl out from a hole in the palm of the hero's hand.

Outrageous, baffling sequences are enlivened with ecstasy, longing and danger. In the first scene a wisp of cloud moves across the full moon; in the second a razor blade cuts through an eye. Physical mutilation and sexual distortion are loosely connected with tango rhythms and Wagner's music from *Tristan und Isolde,* and connected by a haphazard chronology into what were supposed to be rational episodes.

In Dalí's pictures from this period (*Honey is Sweeter than Blood, Male Figure and Female Figure, Gadget and Hand* – also known as *The Birth of Venus*) biographers and art critics claim to see allusions to the act of masturbation. Ian Gibson is very keen to reduce Dalí's works to symbols of his life story but it is always difficult to determine to what extent an artist's life relates to his work. Dalí often described a state in which it was impossible for him to transcend himself – a state of simultaneous desire and seclusion – and how when painting he could give form to this urge. The desire to interact with reality became a major motive for painting and the vivid imagery of the resultant works is in any case above and beyond any encoded expression of his need to masturbate and the pleasure he derived from doing so.

Dalí was obviously disappointed with his second visit to Paris. Unfortunately he was suffering from a cold and there was no one there to mother him. He did nothing and felt like a failure. He met Joan Miró, who advised him to get himself formal clothes, the poet Paul Éluard (born Eugène Grindel), whose verses he admired, Robert Desnos, who offered to buy his painting *First Days of Spring,* and the gallery-owner Goemans, who wanted to exhibit his paintings. He worked on the film with Buñuel and made a histrionic appearance in a priest's vestments, sitting on a piano with corpses of donkeys. However, none of this made him feel he had particularly distinguished himself.

A few days before *Un Chien Andalou* had its premiere in front of an invited audience at the Studio des Ursulines on 6 June 1929 he escaped to his Catalonian retreat. Buñuel reported on its great success by letter. The Vicomte Charles de Noailles and his wife Marie-Laure, leading Parisian art patrons, were particularly taken by the film. They collected avant-garde works and were prepared to finance another film from Buñuel's and Dalí's imaginative world.

Dalí came back to Cadaqués, happy to be home again but in a curious state. Looking back, he believed he had never been nearer to going mad and spoke of hallucinations and compulsive obsessions. He focused on experimenting with this experience, in which images were evoked as though in hypnotic states of trance and meditation. *After having surrendered for a while to these fantasies, which derived from childhood memories, I finally resolved to tackle a painting in which I would confine myself exclusively to reproducing each image as conscientiously as I could, in keeping with the sequence and intensity of their occurrence, and to taking those feelings which came to me completely involuntarily as the criterion and norm for determining the order of the images. [...] This work was one of the most authentic and fundamental to which surrealism could rightly lay claim.*[76] The poet Paul Éluard gave it a title which Dalí liked: *The Lugubrious Game.* (It is also known as *Dismal Sport.*)

His presence in Paris cannot have been as ineffectual he said in his *Secret Life*, for in August of that year René Magritte and his wife, Camille Goemans with his girl-friend and Paul Éluard with his daughter and wife, whom he called Gala, came to Cadaqués for a holiday to be with Dalí. Shortly afterwards Buñuel arrived as well to work with him on a screenplay for the new film, which under the title *L'Age d'Or* was to become both celebrated and notorious.

Dalí described his extravagantly costumed quick-change appearances and how he 'suffered' from fits of laughter. He had an idée fixe, an insistent fantasy, that someone had a wooden owl on their head, which in turn was wearing a pile of his own faeces on its head. Unfortunately his new surrealist friends did not find this at all funny and viewed the young painter with displeasure. They were also uneasy about the underpants with brown stains on them worn by a figure in the painting *The Lugubrious Game*. The surrealists' declared intention not to shy away from any taboo subject apparently met certain limits when it was visibly put into action.

The arrival of Gala, born Helena Diakonov Devulina in Russia, was to have a lasting effect on Dalí's life. He had finally met the woman who could draw the narcissist in him out of the privacy of his visions and into reality. *Gala, you are real, I often said, and held fast the experience of feeling her body.*[77] His love for Gala gave wings to his sexuality as it did to his painting. She did not return to Paris until September.

*For a whole month I shut myself in my studio in Figueres and returned to my familiar monastic life. I completed the portrait of Paul Éluard which I had begun during the summer and two large paintings, of which one was to become famous. On it I put a large, waxy-pale head with bright pink cheeks, long eyelashes and an imposing nose pressing on the ground. This face had no mouth, but a gigantic grasshopper hanging in its place. The putrid stomach of the grasshopper was full of ants, many of which were scurrying around the place where the mouth of this terrifying face should actually have been and the head finished in buildings and ornaments in fin de siècle style.* The painting was called *The Great Masturbator*[78] and was sent with the other paintings in a wooden crate to Paris, where it was shown in Goemans's gallery from 20 November to 5 December.

In spite of its title, *The Great Masturbator* is not simply a

The Great Masturbator, 1929 (oil on canvas).
Museo Nacional Centro de Arte Reina Sofia, Madrid, Spain

biographical account of a sexual practice but a historical work of art. In 1917 de Chirico had called a geometrical construction with a half-bust of a mannequin on its tip *The Great Metaphysician* and undoubtedly Dalí, being deliberately provocative, removed the metaphysician from his pedestal and put something humanly banal in his place.

André Breton wrote in a foreword to the catalogue of Dalí's first solo exhibition in Paris: 'Perhaps Dalí was the first to push our intellectual windows wide open. [...] Dalí's art – the most hallucinatory ever – presents us with a real threat. Completely new creatures with obviously evil intentions are on the move.' [79] Of the eleven paintings two were already sold before the exhibition opened – *The Accommodation of Desire* to André Breton and *The Lugubrious Game* to the Vicomte de Noailles.

Dalí took no part in the opening of his exhibition, perhaps out of shyness but perhaps because he also hoped that feigning indifference would enhance its effect. In any case he was following his principle of deviating from behaviour which would normally be expected. He spent two months with Gala in the Hotel du Château in Carry-le-Rouet on the Côte d'Azur. When they learnt that Goemans had gone bankrupt, Gala went back to Paris to try to recover the money owed to Dalí, while he accepted an invitation from the Vicomte de Noailles to stay at the Abbaye de Saint Bernard near Hyère.

Breton regarded Dalí's early surrealist pictures as pioneering, while his family saw in his new works, as in his new life-style, only the detrimental effect of his taking up with the surrealists. His father and sister were angry that the genius they admired was of all things living in sin with Gala, the surrealist muse who had had affairs with Max Ernst, Giorgio de Chirico, René Char and others. Furthermore, she was a married woman with a child. They hated her.

When Dalí's father learnt through the Spanish press that his son had scrawled across one of his paintings 'I often spit with pleasure on my mother's portrait', he summarily threw him out of the house and disinherited him. Dalí slunk away like a beaten dog. Friends lent him money for a taxi to the French frontier and the rail journey to Paris. Throughout his life Dalí unswervingly described his relationship with his mother as loving beyond all description and one gets the impression that while among the surrealists he was making great efforts to outdo

In my opinion one should not despise it when someone who gazes fixedly at stains on the wall, cabbage cooking on the fire, clouds or a flowing stream, invents wonderful things. The genius of a painter can then take complete hold of him and he will create compositions of battles between animals and men, of landscapes and monsters, of devils and other fantastical things which will do him honour. (Leonardo da Vinci).

them all in breaking through barriers. He may also have secretly wanted to provoke a drastic severing of the 'Gordian umbilical cord' which bound him to his family. In any case, he now had to make his own way in the world.

Dalí and Gala soon after their wedding

Gala Éluard was also taking a decisive step in her life by abandoning her husband and her daughter Cécile, though she remained on friendly terms with the former. They still had sexual intercourse and supported each other financially. In his numerous love letters to Gala[80] Éluard even sent cordial greetings to 'little Dary' (his nickname for Salvador). He admired Dalí's sharp intellect and sometimes invited him to comment on his own poems, welcoming his views with gratitude. Above all he succeeded in getting Dalí to collaborate on the surrealists' journal *Minotaure*, invited him to contribute to it and undertook to include reproductions of his paintings.

Some years later, in 1934, Gala and Salvador married. She was ten years older than him and immediately became a substitute for his family – negotiating sales, agreeing contracts, helping to organise and manage exhibitions, learning how to mix paints and banishing the spectre of his impotence. She sensed that living with Dalí would create new opportunities for herself, while for his part the young artist virtually moulded himself to her, thus creating a happy symbiosis which, in spite of her countless love affairs, lasted almost throughout their lives. No one else was ever to come so close to Dalí and from then on anyone wanting to contact him had to go through Gala. She protected and sheltered him, so that he could dedicate himself wholly to painting, and that was exactly what he wanted.

His basic obsessions were centred around Gala, public self-dramatisation and painting. Gala encouraged his efforts to develop his own version of surrealist art, in order to prove that she had chosen the best, the cleverest, the most talented, the most individual and – as she believed – the only non-bourgeois among the surrealists. It was therefore in her interests to free Dalí from the patronage of André Breton, the doyen of the surrealists. She also played a major part in making him the most financially successful of them all.

For his part, Dalí was ready to tell the whole world how important Gala was to him – and did so in the most spectacular way. He repeatedly declared in public that without her he would be nothing and for a while he signed his pictures 'Gala Salvador Dalí', which is curiously moving, when one remembers that his dead brother was called Salvador Galo Anselmo Dalí.

They now went about everywhere as a couple. Whenever they were in Paris between 1930 and 1932 they lived in the apartment in Rue Becquerel which Éluard had prepared for a new start to their marriage, when he was afraid that Gala was going to leave him. In July 1932 the couple moved to a small studio in the Rue Gauget. In 1932 they conceived an ingenious plan to secure a minimum amount to live on and succeeded in getting together a group of twelve supporters (the so-called 'zodiac'), each of whom would put an agreed sum of money at their disposal for one month a year and in return have the right to one of Dalí's new works.[81]

De Noailles also helped Dalí with a small amount of money to purchase a fisherman's hut on the shore in a fishing village called Port Lligat. At that time there was only a path along the jagged cliffs which was difficult to negotiate, so that it was easier to approach the village from the sea. Dalí needed the atmosphere of his childhood both for living and for painting and the hut protected the artist's vulnerable psyche, like a carapace around a primitive crustacean.

As their lives blossomed and diversified over the years, they added to the number and size of the rooms. *We found a carpenter and Gala and I together designed all the details, from the number of steps in the staircase to the measurements of the smallest windows. Ludwig II of Bavaria did not give half as much thought to his palaces as we did to our little hut. It consisted of a room about four metres square which served us as dining room, bedroom, studio and hallway.*[82] The cottage had been found for them by Lidia Nogués, a fisherman's wife from Cadaqués, who had impressed other people besides Dalí. *Lidia had the most wonderful paranoiac intelligence I have ever met, apart from my own. She was capable of making completely coherent associations between any object you pleased and something which had just come into her head [...].*[83]

Dalí's essays and poems, which appeared from 1930 on in various surrealist periodicals, were not intellectual buffoonery but criticisms of the bourgeois view of spiritual associations. They were essentially concerned with his *Declaration of the Independence of Imagination and [...] of Man's Right to his Own Madness.*[84] His writings were ambitious both linguistically, as literature and as theoretical analysis. They should be viewed as attempts to delve into spiritual states which exist beyond what are generally accepted as 'normal' laws. He wanted to lift the veil off what was considered 'self-evident' reality.

Breton and Éluard, who valued these contributions, wrote: 'The deplorable intellectual evasion hidden behind the word "reality" is today the object of systematic denunciation, which will unquestionably have revolutionary consequences.' [85] The target of the attack was the bourgeois world with its crass censorship mechanism, which was both conscious and subconscious.

As with Feuerbach, Nietzsche, Freud and other thinkers, this was connected with a psychological attitude to observing and questioning. Thus Dalí did not judge Lidia's experiences and reactions as morbid, but enquired what actually happened if one perceived reality as she did. In clinical terms this would be called paranoia.

The French psychiatrist and psychoanalyst Jacques Lacan contacted Dalí through Breton, to talk to him about his essay 'The Donkey's Corpse' (1930) and in 1932 wrote in a dissertation [86] that paranoiacs were unable to perceive the things around them dispassionately; that things were not accessible to them as neutral objects but assumed the character of living entities (usually of a threatening kind), as they do in a child's mentality. Paranoiacs lacked the essential prerequisite of dealing with things rationally and the way in which they controlled their own reality led to special 'plastic and poetic emanations […]. This kind of raving,' he wrote, 'which is often on a par with the inspiration of great artists, […] is actually very fertile in creating recurring illusions, in incessantly multiplying and in continually returning to the same events in doubled and trebled form […]. Such experiences are clearly related to very consistent creative processes in poetry […].' [87]

Dalí wanted to show in his paintings how this kind of illusory perception could be developed by applying what he called the *paranoiac-critical method*, in order to create a new image of reality. His own visual experience was that at best unambiguous figures and associations fleetingly show an interaction with spiritual processes, which change, regroup and reveal ancillary meanings. According to him ambiguity, paradoxical associations and vague ambivalence make up the core of our relationship with reality. We exclude these factors from our everyday thinking, which is governed by arbitrary standards of normality, and attitudes which deviate from them are regarded in western culture as sick or crazy. Surrealism opposed this restrictive interpretation forced on us and applied its own method, which was 'displacement'. Automatism (Breton's psychoanalytical term for giving free rein to invention) deactivated our consciously self-imposed control of our impulses and made room for a kind of spiritual self-regulation.

Dalí envisaged yet another way, an *antagonism between both these kinds of confusion [...]; on the one side the passive confusion of automatism and on the other the active, systematic confusion visualised through the phenomenon of paranoia.*[88] The resulting paradox he called *concrete irrationality,*[89] to be exemplified in *as approximate as possible a realisation of illusory objects designed to [...] collide with those in our daily lives in the bright glare of reality.*[90] So 'object art', was born, related to 'objets trouvés', to Duchamp's 'ready-mades' and to the innovative combination of everyday objects which was later adopted and transformed by pop art.

Even Dalí's appearances at the surrealists' meetings were manifestations of these extraordinary shifts between differing levels of reality. You could never be sure whether his contributions to the conversation were meant seriously or whether his irrelevant remarks in highly theoretical discussions were simply intended to needle Breton, the lofty 'pontifex'. As in his dealings with his father or with his art teachers in Madrid, Dalí loved to be playfully and aggressively provocative.

André Thirion recalled that Dalí with his 'inexhaustible gift of the gab [...] was clearly capable of ruining any sort of intellectual construct, simply because he was so superbly funny'. Dalí guessed that Breton was no match for his kind of ebullience, and that egged him on. In his painting *The Enigma of William Tell* he overstepped the mark; it 'showed a kneeling Lenin with a grotesquely elongated peak to his cap and a naked right buttock as long and limp as a soggy baguette'.[91]

Dalí was opposed to the surrealists' differentiation between political and religious morality and rejected their overwhelming orientation towards Communism. By 'surreally' talking about Hitler's paranoiac potential, the beauty of his plump back and the astonishing quantity of his testicles, Dalí was attacking Breton's embargo on applying to political affairs the surrealist vision that widely differing dimensions of the same subject matter could be viewed simultaneously.

On 5 February 1934 Breton called Dalí to account before the group of surrealists. 'Claiming to have a high temperature, Dalí kept a thermometer in his mouth throughout the session. Breton [...] summarised the group's complaints against him.'[92] It was soon clear that Dalí was successfully making a spectacle out of the situation. Dripping with sweat and wearing far too many sweaters, he kept taking off his jacket to remove yet another pullover and pulling 'a bundle of papers out of his pocket – a sort of jumble of manifesto and defence speech – he began to read. He interrupted himself repeatedly to pull up his socks, take off another garment and read the thermometer. [...] When he finally declared that Hitler had "four balls and six foreskins", Breton broke in brusquely to ask: "Are you going to bore us for much longer with your Hitler?" [...] However, [...] Dalí [...] soon showed he was in control of the situation. His comic accent and the spittle which flew into Breton's face while he was speaking because of the thermometer [...] undermined the atmosphere Breton had wanted to create for the occasion. [...] Dalí then referred to Breton's own standards from the first "manifesto" and asserted that he was simply clinging to his dreams as faithfully as possible – irrespective of whether they were about Gala, Dulita, de Sade or Hitler. "So, my dear Breton", he finished imperiously, "If I dream tonight that I am screwing you, tomorrow morning I shall paint all our best fucking positions in the greatest detail." Breton was now bereft of speech and just burst out in icy anger: "I wouldn't advise you to, my friend." '[93]

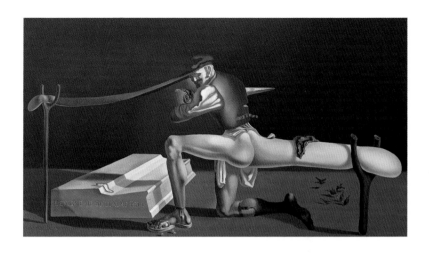

The Enigma of William Tell , 1934 (second version)

The Marx Brothers could not have invented a funnier scene. Breton subsequently expelled Dalí from the surrealists' association, but this did not prevent them from collaborating later in organising exhibitions.

Obsessed, Dalí continued to sketch out his insoluble riddles, which capture the spectator's attention and keep it moving through a quantity of different perspectives – for instance, when a woman turns first into a horse and then into a lion. [94] At first glance these inventions look like trompes l'oeil (Müller-Lyer) which to psychologists demonstrate that a special psychodynamic determines our dealings with supposedly objective physical reality. *Through an unmistakably paranoiac process it has become possible to obtain a double image: that is, to portray something which, without the slightest change in its figuration or anatomy, simultaneously represents something completely different, but if also free from any distortion or anomaly whatever which might give the impression of its having been pre-arranged.* [95]

Dalí's multiple or puzzle pictures are based on 16th- and 17th-century tradition and he even quoted Arcimboldo, Bracelli and others. A more recent predilection came from Odilon Redon: 'The feeling of mystery is always present in things with many facets, in double or triple aspects, in hints of aspects (images within images) and in forms which develop or begin to develop, according to the intellectual disposition of the spectator.'[96]

In his essays Dalí calculated that these were verbal realisations of *latent intentions* and simultaneously of the *power of the concrete*, both of which *are almost always suppressed* in the waking state. The *concretely irrational* appears in his paintings and writings as in his films.[97]

Integration and metamorphosis do not only apply to 'fantasy images', but to associations in reality such as 'within and without', and 'turning and folding',[98] as well as to convulsive visions of ruin, beauty and horror, pan-sexuality, inversion and distortion, which Hocke had claimed for mannerism.[99] In both his painting and his theorising Dalí revealed a vision of reality which he called 'morphology', at the core of which lay transformation, ambiguity, analogy and echo. 'Like Leonardo, he tries to morphologise everything.'[100]

Dalí's works were impressing an ever-widening circle of private collectors, dealers and art-lovers and, through an introduction from the Vicomte de Noailles, the Paris dealer Pierre Colle signed a contract with him in June 1930, by which he would organise exhibitions and find him buyers. At a dinner he was introduced by the Vicomte to Alfred Barr, director of the Museum of Modern Art (MOMA) which had opened in New York in 1929, and to René Crevel, who wrote about Dalí's anti-obscurantism and in turn introduced him to Caresse Crosby. She and her husband had founded the Black Sun Press in Paris to publish works by the artistic avant garde. Dalí and Gala quickly joined their circle of friends and were often guests at the Moulin de Soleil, their country house to the north of Paris.

America was already looming on his horizon. *This was a period when Cole Porter's* Night and Day *moaned continuously from the gramophone and for the first time in my life I looked through* The New Yorker *and* Town and Country *magazines. I seized at every picture from America with the sort of voraciousness with which one greets the first hint of a smell emanating from a sensational repast which one is about to enjoy.*[101]

Julien Levy, who was exhibiting surrealist works in his New York gallery in 1932 – among them three paintings by Dalí – helped to introduce him to the New World. Avid to make his mark and in need of money, his alienation from the surrealists contributed to his search for pastures new. In February 1934 he exhibited *The Enigma of William Tell* in the Salon des Indépendants; he was trying to bring his 'work into direct contact with a wide public and with life itself' [102] and not just travel in the slipstream of the surrealists. The illustrations to Lautréamont's *Songs of Maldoror* (drawings and graphics) which he made for the publisher Skira were shown by Julien Levy in New York and the Carnegie Institute in Pittsburgh included his painting *Landscape with Enigmatic Elements* in its 1934 International Exhibition of Paintings, where it was particularly well received by the critics.

A further exhibition of paintings in the Galerie Jacques Bonjean in Paris was greeted with high praise by the critic Louis Chéronnet in *Art et Décoration*: 'Dante had no more cosmic fantasy than this painter and the Musée Dupuytren contains no more horrors than are to be found in these works. And yet, as soon as you reach this shore on which, entirely isolated and apparently independent of one another, bleached bones are stranded, limp bodies teem with obscene insects and objects

Portrait of Gala Balancing Two Lamb Chops on her Shoulders, 1933 (oil on canvas). Museo Dalí, Figueres, Spain

decay in blazing heat – heat so vividly portrayed that it seems tangible to feverish fingers – or this island of the dead with its constantly sunny weather, monumental cypresses and perverse gaiety: then a strange magic exerts its spell over you […].' [103]

Compressing, stretching to the limits, crumbling away, fragmenting, montage, density, merging, fading, isolating, shading over, contrasting, hollowing out, expanding and contracting, making transitory and repeating were methods which so intensified and sharpened the effect of Dalí's paintings that viewers could relate to them through familiarity with their own dreams and with images they recall of sudden occurrences, such as earthquake, love or war. These paintings draw the viewers into an irritatingly vague and shifting experience which can elevate and liberate their everyday selves.

In a one-man show at the Zwemmer Gallery in London the English public had a chance to see some of Dalí's pictures and prints, which Zwemmer had recently acquired. Douglas Goldring judged the contents as 'simultaneously surprising and revolutionary. It is rare for me to want to pay a return visit to an exhibition. I must admit that this one exerted a deep fascination on me.'[104]

In 1934 Dalí summoned the courage to cross the Atlantic for the first time, accompanied by Gala, Caresse Crosby and his pictures, Picasso having apparently lent him money for the fare. Of their arrival in New York Caresse Crosby wrote: 'For journalists looking for copy Dalí was really worth attention, as he had […] tied himself to his pictures. "They want to see some of your work", I explained to him, "These are the gentlemen of the press" […]. He got the idea at once […] and began stripping the paper from the largest and most unwieldy of the paintings. The first they found puzzling and the second made them shake with laughter. […] When they asked Dalí which was his favourite painting, he answered: "The portrait of my wife". "Yes", I agreed, "you see, he has painted her with lamb chops on her shoulders." "Lamb chops?" they all roared. That did it! The pencils began to move, the cameras to click.'[105]

Dalí recalled: *To them I was a king of fools, a clown and a mountebank; none of them had grasped the pent-up strength and Nietzschean will-power which lay behind my outward appearance.*[106] The *New York Evening Journal* printed a photograph of Gala and Salvador Dalí in their midday edition with the caption: 'From lamb chops to art'.[107]

On 21 November Julien Levy opened his first Dalí solo exhibition, which was very enthusiastically received and at which twelve paintings were sold. The art critics hailed Dalí as one of the greatest – controversial, difficult, an outstanding draughtsman – and for the next two months he was a living publicity campaign for surrealism. Some 200 curious art-lovers came to his exhibition at the Wadsworth Atheneum in Hartford, Connecticut, which he enlivened with a slide-lecture and a showing of the film *Un Chien Andalou.*

On 11 January 1935 he gave a lecture in French at the MOMA, entitled 'Surrealist Paintings and Paranoiac Images', and illustrated it with some of his own pictures, 17th-century prints and paintings by Picasso and Max Ernst. His central thesis was: *The subconscious has a symbolic language that is a truly universal language, for it does not depend on a special habitude or state of culture or intelligence, but speaks with the vocabulary of the great, vital constants – sexual instinct, feeling of death, physical notion of the enigma of space – these vital constants are universally echoed in every human.*[108]

Dalí's workload was prodigious – he made contacts, found opportunities for exhibitions and organised them. He was always on the move, publicising himself and living a restless life full of grand climaxes.

In Cadaqués in 1936 he was movingly reconciled with his father, who revised his will in favour of his son, though he later changed it again in favour of Ana Maria.

One exhibition followed another – including the International Surrealist Exhibition in the New Burlington Galleries in London on 11 June 1936 – while as a sideline Dalí was continuing to illustrate literary texts and write essays like 'All Honour to the Object', 'The Spectral Surrealism of the Pre-Raphaelite Eternal Female' or 'The First Law of Morphology concerning Hair in soft Structures' – texts in which he was consolidating his vision as a painter with surrealist principles.

From then on writing joined with painting as an expressive

medium for Dalí and in it he followed the same principles of displacement, condensation, montage and collage of images and ideas, quick changes between vagueness and photographically concrete reality and sudden leaps between psychological perceptions and surrealist exaggeration. The effect on the reader is like brainwashing, making it nearly impossible to determine whether one is being offered carefully devised practical jokes or new insights into unfamiliar phenomena.

Among the many people he met in the late 1930s, the English multi-millionaire, poet and dandy Edward James was particularly important in Dalí's life. He became his patron and close friend and in 1936 acquired a contractual right to Dalí's artistic output for the next four years. With this cosmopolitan man Dalí travelled to Italy, where he studied classical Italian painting and became enthusiastic about Raphael and the mannerists.

In June 1936 Dalí went to London for a 'lecture-happening', for which he wore a diving suit (and nearly suffocated in it), because he wanted to personify the exploration of the depths of the unconscious inherent in surrealist painting. On 7 December he was back in New York for his second solo exhibition at Julien Levy's gallery, where all the paintings were sold on the opening day, and then exhibited six further paintings in the first exhibition of dada and surrealist art organised by Alfred Barr at the MOMA, entitled 'Fantastic Art, Dada and Surrealism'.

In February 1937 Dalí went to Hollywood, where he met the Marx Brothers whom he regarded as surrealists. He painted a portrait of Harpo Marx playing a harp with barbed-wire strings and spoons for decoration and sketched a scenario for a film which was never made. Hollywood and surrealism did not go together. In April 1937 he and Gala spent a holiday in the Swiss and Austrian mountains, where snow was still lying and he was bored to death. In Spain the Civil War was raging and Dalí was deeply disturbed by a report that 30 people had been shot in Cadaqués.

Dalí had long wanted to meet Sigmund Freud, who was living in exile in London, and Edward James and Stefan Zweig arranged for him to do so on 19 July 1938. Dalí convulsively harangued the octogenarian in his well-nigh unintelligible English, using the *Metamorphosis of Narcissus* to explain how surrealist painting gave visible form to the unconscious. He also made a sketch of the head of the great founder of psychoanalysis who, together with Nietzsche and Marx, became one of the pioneers of modern thought. 'Until I met Dalí', wrote Freud to Stefan Zweig, 'I was inclined to consider the surrealists, who seemed to have elected me their patron saint, as absolute fools (or maybe 95 percent, as in alcohol). The young Spaniard with his sincere, fanatical eyes and indisputable technical mastery persuaded me to revise my opinion.' [109]

Many of the works Dalí painted in the 1930s initiated in his viewers a process of perception which resulted in their experiencing infinity in space and time. They virtually 'saw' the paradox of the eternal moment – an effect similar to that of works by the American painter Edward Hopper. Though otherwise working quite differently, these two artists both imbued enigmas with mystery and used the impossibility of harmony as one of their themes. While Hopper's effectiveness was actually related to his lack of artistry, Dalí showed brilliant, perfect taste in his treatment of colours and draughtsmanship. He was unequalled in his portrayal of the bizarre nature of obscure objects, the sparks flying between disparate elements, the precision of the soft and the amorphous, the labyrinthine character and the richly detailed, but nonetheless monumental, element in surrealist invention.

Flat application of colour in the style of the Old Masters is a characteristic of Dalí's painting. Colour does not figure in his works as a material with a physical volume, as it does in those of Van Gogh. He had his own particular way of combining displacement of large and small objects, inverting, stretching and shrinking, repeating, quoting himself, making mirror images and double imagery, hollowing-out, turning around and creating analogies between figures as vehicles for his transformations (morphology).

Between 1929 and 1939 Dalí executed some 700 oil paintings, mostly in a small format, which represent about half of his entire output.[110] To this decade belong the pictorial elements familiar to everyone – fried eggs, soft watches, Wilhelm Tell, girls jumping over ropes, a small boy with a hoop, a pine tree, figures taken from Millet, outsize telephone receivers, lobsters, Gala, Venus with drawers, ants, burning giraffes and long-legged elephants. People have called them the pictorial encoding of ideas or, more grandly, a sort of mythology which can be related to his private life. Some of his own explanations do of course encourage us to make such a correlation but he did challenge the claim that the meaning of his pictures should be immediately apparent to everyone. *How can you expect the public to understand the meaning of the images I transcribe when I myself – the person who created them – no longer understand them once they appear in my paintings?*[111]

Art historians, critics and amateur art-lovers all rate Dalí's paintings from his classical surrealist phase in the late 1920s and the 1930s particularly highly. These works have enhanced his fame and rival those of his later periods in the eyes of experts (though not of buyers), and they alone appear in anthologies of 20th-century art, which might lead people to suppose that the artist had reached his peak at an early age and died around 1940.

# Shaman of the moderns: transatlantic artfulness (1939-1948)

History proves that an artist can create significant works and yet only be famous posthumously. (Vincent Van Gogh is a pitiable example.) Out of his fate modern opinion has created a definitive legend of an artist's life: incapable of organising his daily existence, struggling with God, men and angels, ignored, selling nothing in his lifetime, suffering, freezing and starving. Financial success would seem almost disreputable.

But Dalí was successful in America and Breton was jealous. He made an anagram of 'Salvador Dalí' as 'Avida dollars' (greedy for dollars). Dalí had no problem with being associated with dollars and unhesitatingly adopted Breton's nickname, signed several of his works with it and in 1965 even painted a picture called *The Apotheosis of the Dollar.* Not everyone in America was happy to see how he conquered the art market and someone dubbed him the P T Barnum of painting – referring to the unconventional publicity for Barnum's Circus. Dalí was a modern court jester or post-modern pop star and loved to play games with the media. It was not until the era of pop art in the 1960s that a new image of the artist was formed in the conspicuous figure of Andy Warhol.

For Dalí the idea of suffering the same fate as Van Gogh was out of the question; he wanted to be great in his own lifetime. As a young artist in Spain he had already discovered how effective it was when newspapers and art journals wrote stories about his appearance and his works. He had realised that people and things were not what they were but what you made of them, which applied to artists and their works just as much as to other products, people and events. The American media showed great interest in his penchant for exaggeration, self-dramatisation, extravagant masquerading and abrupt changes of attitude to public opinion – sometimes enthusiastic, sometimes outraged – and he made strategic use of publicity to ensure that he was always in the public eye.[112]

In March 1939 he designed 'Day and Night', a window display for the spring collection of the New York department store Bonwit Teller. When he found that his design had been changed into something more conventionally pleasing, he reacted with fury, demolished it (breaking the window as he did so) and was arrested, which gave the media a field day. In the same year Man Ray's photograph of him appeared on the cover of *Time* magazine with the caption 'Surrealist Salvador Dalí'.[113]

When he set up his *Taxi pluvieux (Rainy Taxi)* at the International Surrealist Exhibition in Paris in 1938, he had chosen an art form which went beyond painting and object art. In April 1939 the *New York Times* reported that he had been commissioned to design a surrealist pavilion for the New York World Exhibition: 'Salvador Dalí, the surrealist painter who recently broke a shop window in Fifth Avenue has, as was reported yesterday, now broken into the entertainment zone of the World Exhibition.' For 25 cents one could watch a three-dimensional show lasting ten to twelve minutes, presented by 'Living Liquid Ladies', or 'splendid female underwater swimmers'. When the organisers decided to censor it, because this *Dream of Venus* seemed to them offensive, he responded with a public commentary which he signed 'Impresario of a Sideshow in the Entertainment Section.'[114] In surrealist fashion Dalí was undermining the traditional divisions between the genres of salon painting, museum art, publicity, design, entertainment art and other forms and invented the 'art spectacle' or 'happening' – a new form of expressing the artist's treatment of reality – which was accepted in the 1960s as an art form in its own right. The *Dream of Venus* was, besides, an 'environment', a sculpture you could walk into, with borrowings from the architect Antoni Gaudí's art nouveau style.

It attracted plenty of publicity and huge crowds flocked to see the exhibition of his paintings in the Julien Levy Gallery between 21 March and 7 April. A particular attraction was *The Endless Enigma* (1938; 114.30 x 144 cm), which Breton had dismissed as a mere visual crossword puzzle. However, even when one knew that Dalí had selected and drafted out set pieces and then effected changes in them by superimposing them on each other, it would be ridiculous to reduce its impact to a mere desire to decipher its structural conundrum. It disturbed and intrigued viewers just because of its complexity and multifarious layers of meaning.

The political situation in Europe was equally confused and complex. In Spain the Republic was tottering and the Civil War had raged there since General Franco's campaign in Spanish Morocco in July 1936. Dalí and Gala had to give up their life in Port Lligat and move their main residence to Paris. The left-wing, supported by volunteers from all over the world, including many intellectuals and artists, fought against the Fascists, whose interests in the Falange party were well organised and shared by the clergy; together they wanted to establish a totalitarian dictatorship. The unbridled force and savagery on both sides resulted in whole villages being razed to the ground. Dalí's sister was held by the Reds for 20 days in Cadaqués; she temporarily lost her reason and had to be fed artificially. Their father's house was ransacked and he himself was threatened. Like many other former Republicans, he had seen a saviour in time of need in Franco and his promise to restore order.

In March 1939 the Republic collapsed. Hitler and Mussolini, who shared Franco's political ideology, had supported him and were now engaged in changing the balance of power in Europe to their advantage through campaigns of conquest. The German troops' invasion of Poland on 1 September 1939 triggered the start of the Second World War.

While Dalí was painting dreamlike visions in his campaign to make people aware of the enigmatic craziness of life, the Fascists were harnessing all their power to establish a so-called racially pure society. They assumed the right to kill and eliminate anything which opposed them; their enemy was not only Communism but any kind of diversity. In exile in America Dalí wrote: *People want […] me to make up my mind whether I am a Stalinist or a Hitlerist. No! […] I would always remain what I was until I died, Dalí and only Dalí! I believed in neither the Communist nor the Nazi Revolution.*[115]

Dalí used the theme of civil war in several paintings –as early as 1936 in a picture entitled *Soft Constructions with Boiled Beans* or *Premonition of War* (100 x 99 cm). Decimated flesh and bone fragments of a decomposed corpse erupt into a jagged sky, resting precariously on a disproportionately small cupboard standing like the centre of a seesaw in the middle of a landscape. This is a monstrous sculptural creation with body parts rearranged in a rectangle. A head with a contorted face and bared teeth is painted like a sort of cliff, stretching to the upper edge of the picture. Rust-brown tones contrast with deep blue, blending through shades of pale, sickly yellowish-green. Hideous bones, hands and feet are depicted like roots or tubers as in many of his other pictures. A hand bizarrely grasps a bodily excrescence, the end of which is formed like a breast. The relationship between large and small is reversed; above another hand at the bottom left is a tiny, helpless-looking man, two-thirds concealed. On rust-red soil are scattered some light-coloured beans, representing basic food. The unwieldy structure is held up by brute force: 'homo erectus' –'From earth you came …'

Soft Construction with Boiled Beans: Premonition of Civil War,
1936 (oil on canvas).
Philadelphia Museum of Art, Pennsylvania, USA

In another picture, *The Enigma of Hitler* (1939; 51.2 x 79.3 cm), Dalí takes the current political situation as his theme, without declaring his own convictions but just presenting a surreally aesthetic vision of an inconceivable occurrence against the background of a landscape in dull grey-blue shades. At first glance the picture is as incomprehensible as the phenomenon of Hitler himself, but if one takes the time to give one's reactions free rein, some kind of meaning does surface. One first notices the wreckage of a dark, outsize telephone receiver, then its combination with a light-coloured plate to form an oval which spreads over the whole width of the picture. An almost obscene drop of saliva is about to fall out of the receiver into the dish standing ready to receive it, where an open husk is lying. Chamberlain's outsize umbrella, war by telephone (a technical device put in a natural setting to form a 'bad connection') – this is menacing, blue horror. [116]

While in Europe in 1939, in the shadow of an image of mankind reduced to the 'pedigree' format of a pure, superior race, madness was being unleashed in the full brutality of war, Dalí in America was writing his *Declaration of the Independence of Imagination and of Man's Right to his own Madness* and had this polemical leaflet dropped from an aeroplane over New York. He had been prohibited from depicting a naked woman with a fish's head in his *Dream of Venus* and this diatribe was apparently intended to persuade American advertisers that they should make more use of poetic elements, but the basic idea went further: he was calling on art to familiarise people with their own irrationality, in order to prevent their being confined within the single dimension of animals – or the bourgeoisie – which, while apparently serving sensible aims, could erupt into the devastating madness of war.

In 1939 the Dalís moved to Arcachon in Southern France, where a number of artists and intellectuals from Germany and other countries had taken refuge from Hitler's troops, among them Marcel Duchamp, Léonor Fini and Coco Chanel. When the Germans occupied France in 1940, Dalí said goodbye to his father in Figueres and went to Lisbon, where Gala had arranged for them to sail to the United States in the *Excambion*.

Dalí's connections in the New World proved extraordinarily helpful. The generous Caresse Crosby let them stay with her at Hampton Manor in Virginia – an American version of the Moulin de Soleil. One fellow-guest was the professional diarist Anaïs Nin, who had also fled from Paris. Just as Gala was promoting Dalí, her painter, Anaïs Nin had taken under her wing the writer and artist Henry Miller, who was financially less successful than Dalí, although he worked just as industriously.

The other guests were not pleased to see Dalí given the starring role in the household, while they were reduced to the status of satellites. Anaïs Nin noted: 'They were both [Gala and Salvador Dalí] short in stature and sat close together. Both were inconspicuous, she rather faded and dressed in muted colours and he like a charcoal drawing, like a child's drawing of a Spaniard, any Spaniard, apart from the incredible length of his moustache. They clung together as though needing protection and comfort and were not open, confident or relaxed.' [117]

Gala distributed errands to the other guests when Dalí needed canvas, paints or paper. 'So we all did our allotted jobs. Mrs Dalí never raised her voice, never pleaded, never charmed us. She just calmly assumed we were all there to serve Dalí, the great and undisputed genius.' [118]

At the age of 37 Dalí was preoccupied by the ambition to advance his career. Exile had interrupted his upward path and called for some revision or rethinking. How should and could his life progress in these circumstances? It was certainly important to continue conquering the American art market, but was that all? Where was the point in generalised defiance, when one was living in a strange country while the world was plunged into chaos by war? He also had to struggle with this awkward language, the sound of which he never mastered. Would the pose he had so far established with his paranoiac-critical visions see him through the rest of his life, in the light of the current state of the world? What had actually been driving him on through all the past tumultuous years?

This time he had not gone to America of his own free will. He did indeed have several commissions to fill but expanding his sphere of influence in America was now hampered by his being cut off from his refuge at Port Lligat. That continuity of experience and wholeness which were automatically guaranteed to him by the simple fact of being at home where he belonged, surrounded by the landscape, language and nature which he could smell, grasp, hear and physically feel, were for the moment at stake. So, far from home, he recalled (in French) his origins, upbringing and childhood in Spain. With humour and linguistic flair he drafted his autobiography *La Vie Secrète de Salvador Dalí* – an account of himself the artist as a 'holy trickster' and a genius.

Dalí traced the relationship to painting of his whole life-story, with its important moments and themes: the impudent, pleasure-seeking child, the sensual body, the ever-indulgent mother, death, the ambivalent relationship with his father, his headstrong craziness, the surrealists, politics, Gala, solitude, public appearances, psychoanalysis, sexuality, dreams and the experience of nature. Few autobiographies bear such sophisticated witness to the development of a fanatical artist.

Dalí spent half a year writing *The Secret Life*, while – almost as a sideline – painting several pictures for his next one-man show at the Julien Levy Gallery from 22 April to 23 May 1941, which was subsequently admired by 1500 visitors in Los Angeles. On the cover of the catalogue is his *Soft Self-portrait with Grilled Bacon*. The catalogue stated that his psychological period was coming to an end, to be followed by a morphological era, characterised by form, control and structure. Dalí invited the public *to his last scandal and the beginning of his classical painting.* [119]

Here was a fresh approach with a change of emphasis – but also a fresh aspiration, which was not immediately apparent in these new works. Without question Dalí was searching for stability and orientation in the current chaotic situation. *The evils of war and revolution into which my country was plunged only increased the whole vehemence of my aesthetic passion and, while my homeland was facing death and destruction, I was consulting that other oracle of the future of Western Europe – the Renaissance. I knew that the whole of Europe would follow Spain into war in the wake of the Communist and Fascist revolutions and that out of poverty and the collapse of collectivist doctrines a medieval epoch*

Salvador Dalí Museum,
St Petersburg, Florida, USA

*would emerge, in which individual, spiritual and religious values would be revived. In these coming Middle Ages I wanted to be the first person poised to pronounce the word 'renaissance' in full understanding of the laws of the life and death of aesthetics.*[120]

After finishing *The Secret Life*, he and Gala went to Pebble Beach in California in July 1941 and stayed in the luxury Del Monte Lodge on favourable terms, because Dalí's presence there was seen as good publicity. This was a smart move and in September the Dalís gave a benefit banquet for emigrant artists. 'Clark Gable, Bob Hope, Bing Crosby and Ginger Rogers flew in from Hollywood, the Hitchcocks and a sprinkling of millionaires came from New York. A radiant Gala presided with Dalí over a long table piled with allegedly surrealist bric-à-brac.'[121]

In Carmel Dalí found a studio where he worked on designs for the ballet 'Labyrinth', an adaptation of the myth of Theseus and Ariadne, which had its premiere at the Metropolitan Opera in New York by the Ballets Russes de Monte Carlo on 8 October. Libretto, sets and costumes were by Dalí, the choreography by Leonide Massine and the music was Schubert's.

On 18 November a large-scale retrospective exhibition of the two Spanish surrealists Dalí and Miró opened at the MOMA, with over 40 Dalí paintings and 17 of his drawings. The exhibition 'offered a truly comprehensive overview [...], from cubism to his "gadgets", from surrealism to complex pictures, from drawers to telephones. It travelled to eight major cities – Los Angeles,

Chicago, Cleveland, Palm Beach, San Francisco, Cincinnati, Pittsburgh and Santa Barbara and spread Dalí's fame throughout America. He was beginning to earn real money.' [122]

The first painting he executed in America, *Daddy Long Legs of the Evening – Hope!,* was the founding item in what was to become the most comprehensive Dalí collection ever. Reynolds and Eleanor Morse, a young husband and wife from Denver, Colorado, who owned a factory supplying equipment to the plastic injection moulding industry, had seen his works in friends' houses and also in Cleveland and been captivated by them. Out of their amateur enthusiasm grew a passion, then a strategy for collecting and finally a life-style: travelling with the Dalís, helping to mount exhibitions, translating some of his writings, visiting Port Lligat and writing monographs on his works.

In private Dalí was a very considerate man, said Eleanor Morse, with a quick understanding and an incredible fund of knowledge. She found his transformation into a poseur as soon as the press arrived quite astonishing. Dalí apparently liked her and her husband because they were so much younger than other collectors and Eleanor, through this friendship with Dalí, was able to fulfil her devotion to the arts. She had studied singing, partly in Italy, but had given up the prospects of a professional career when she married. Today the Morses' collection is open to the public in the Salvador Dalí Museum in St Petersburg, Florida, which they founded in 1982. [123]

Being familiar with Italian Renaissance painting, the Morses particularly enjoyed the influence of the old masters on Dalí. His pictures were also very affordable; the first one only cost them $600. Dalí asked whether they wanted the frame, saying it was genuine Renaissance, and they had to pay almost twice as much to include it in the purchase. [124]

Dalí's output was in full swing. At the Julien Levy Gallery he had already exhibited jewellery and vases, followed by a series of pieces of jewellery in neo-Renaissance style, some of which were executed by Carlos Alemany. Dalí designed jewellery with the Duc de Verdura, fitted out Helena Rubinstein's apartment, worked regularly with prominent magazines like *Vogue, Harper's Bazaar* and *Town and Country* and directed ballets, for which he also designed the sets and costumes – *El Café de Chinitas* (García Lorca), *Colloque Sentimental* (after Paul Verlaine, with music by Paul Bowles) and *Tristan Fou* (later renamed *Bacchanale*). He illustrated Maurice Sandoz's *The Fantastic Memories*, also *Le Labyrinthe* and *Benvenuto Cellini's Autobiography*. He wrote his first novel *Hidden Faces* in just a few weeks while staying with the Marquis de Cuevas in New Hampshire, in 1943 he designed the publicity for Schiaparelli's perfume 'Shocking' and publicised himself with a photo-reportage in the magazine 'Click'. He also mounted an exhibition of portraits of American celebrities in the Knoedler Gallery in New York. [125] These almost photographic, hyper-realistic portraits of American high society were set against typically surreal Dalí landscapes embellished with references to previous paintings.

*Hidden Faces* described with baroque verbosity the world of European aristocracy in the 1930s and 1940s. The various long drawn-out episodes (the book runs to over 300 pages) are held together somewhat flimsily through the love of Solange de Cléda for Count Grandsailles. The Count pursues love affairs with other women and ends, willynilly, by marrying one of them. Clé-Dalí, a figure fascinated by death and decay, finds solace in day-dreaming.

The book is tedious and the question is whether it is really worth the effort to read it through. Its only interest lies in the impression that Dalí is using his characters to express his own current view of life. The Civil War pilot Baba says: '[…] Even I believe again in the inextinguishable power of tradition and aristocracy and today I feel my revolutionary illusions from the days of the Spanish Civil War were remote seeds of what I have already reaped in my life. A new desire for the clear-cut and the dependable is taking hold of us; […] I want to return to the nobility of naked feet placed firmly on the ground. I know now that a man must look up humbly towards heaven. You see, this war has made me a Catholic.' [126]

This is one strand in the text, another being introduced with the invented word 'CléDalism' in his foreword. Is this a *roman à clef*? The author was dealing with the 'key' to Dalism. His protagonist Solange de Cléda and her behaviour were to invent a new 'ism'. De Sade had given names to sadism and masochism (respectively, the pleasure gained from inflicting pain on a subject and that of suffering pain at the subject's hands). *CléDalism is both pleasure and pain, sublimated in an all-pervading identification with the subject.* [127]

This is psychologically interesting as self-analysis but difficult to follow through the labyrinthine plot. However, if one relates it to Dalí the man, one can guess at the ideas he is trying to convey. Lacan described illusion as a state in which a person is unable to dissociate him or herself from things and people. Dalí does not fit the mould of an artist who, god-like, wilfully fashions mundane raw material after his own image; he is driven far more by the basic experience of living under the spell of things and people in a symbiotic, inseparable relationship, at their mercy and overpowered.

If one observes his fluid movements (look at any of his many television appearances), one gets the impression that if he were a substance like wax, he would be open to manipulation by any person or thing which came in contact with him.

We can understand Gala's extraordinary importance for him in the context of his self-interpretation. In the book 'Comment on devient Dalí' (*The Unspeakable Confessions of Salvador Dalí*) he wrote: *[…] I had no contours. I was nothing and yet everything,*

*[…] I floated uncertainly and vaguely. My body and soul lived in softness and ambivalence and I existed in things as much as in landscapes. My psychological space was not crystallised in a body but rather dissolved within infinite space [...].*[128] Being in contrast somewhat hard, decisive and cold, Gala was his shell or armour. *Gala has given me in the truest sense of the word the structure which was lacking in my life.* [129] His withdrawal into a strict work routine (he was a workaholic) also gave him a protection against this dissolution.

Once again he threw himself into a new project – this time a film. The Dalís had bought a Cadillac, with windows of two-tone glass specially made to his design, which they drove from the East Coast to the West and back. In Hollywood in 1944 Hitchcock was making the first psychoanalytical film *Spellbound* – on the 'story of a madman who seizes control of an asylum',[130] in which the nurses are also mad. Hitchcock reported: 'I worked with Ben Hecht, who had been treated by a number of psychoanalysts. When we came to the dream sequence, I was determined to break with the tradition of cinematic dreams, which are usually misty and distorted, with fluttering images and so on. I asked Selznick to engage Salvador Dalí to work with us. Selznick agreed, but I am sure he thought I had only done it for the publicity. My sole reason was to create purely visual dreams, with clear-cut outlines, harder than the images in the film itself. I wanted Dalí for the sharp contours of his pictures (de Chirico is very similar) and for the long shadows, the infinite distances, the fleeting lines which meet at infinity and the formless faces.' [131] Dalí went to work immediately and designed the images they wanted. In the cutting room some scenes were taken out and others arbitrarily altered, which angered Hitchcock as much as it did Dalí. But that's how Hollywood works.

A joint venture with Walt Disney, who liked the dream scenes so much that he wanted to engage Dalí for the graphic pas-

Dalí and Hitchcock

sages in his film *Destino*, came to nothing, because the Hollywood moguls were not keen on surrealism. However, Dalí got on well with Disney, who was enthusiastic about his prolific inventiveness and later paid him a visit in Port Lligat.

Shortly after finishing work on *Spellbound* Dalí went to New York to prepare his exhibition at the Bignou Gallery: eleven paintings and a quantity of water-colours, drawings and illustrations, among them designs for Cervantes's *Don Quixote*. He also produced a brochure called *Dalí News, Monarch of the Dailies*. He loved playing games with his name and with the media. He was probably the first artist to dramatise himself as front-page news in his own spoof newspaper.[132] Every line in the four-page brochure was about Dalí's doings, plans and marvels and like any self-respecting newspaper it had its advertising: *Do you suffer 'Periodic' Intellectual Misery? Esthetic depression, fatigue, disgust of life, manic depression, congenital mediocrity, gelatinous cretinism, diamond stones in the kidneys, impotence, frigidity? TAKE 'DALINAL', THE ARTIFICIAL FIRE OF THE SPIRIT WHICH WILL STIMULATE YOU AGAIN.*[133]

After the war in Europe was over, the Americans dropped the first atomic bomb on Hiroshima in August 1945 and the second on Nagasaki three days later. Dalí was as shattered by these events as was everyone else. In his painting *Melancholy. Atomic, Uranic Idyll* (1945; 65 x 85 cm), exhibited by Bignou, Dalí chose the sombre tones of melancholy – a dark-grey space in which everything is loose and suspended, rising or sinking, as in a nightmare. The *Face of War* (1940/41; 64 x 79 cm), however, has the familiar glowing colours of most of his other paintings. Cut into the upper edge of the picture against a bright landscape is a soft, monumental head, its brow furrowed with care, with wide open eyes and a gaping, screaming mouth filled with three skulls, the eyes and mouths of which are filled with more skulls and so on.

Dalí's painting style was widely criticised at the time. Some viewers disliked the detail, because it left nothing to the imagination, some found his pictures too convoluted, others suspected them of being kitsch and the surrealists accused him of betraying their vision. Many people reproached him for the superficiality of his new works, saying that they were too smooth, almost polished and that besides, he was bereft of ideas, as witnessed by his repeating his pictorial inventions from the 1930s. Gibson called them stereotypes or symbols of specific significance. Some reviews read like dictionaries of dream symbolism but do not lead to any real understanding of either the meaning of the dreams or why these works had such impact.

In 1948 Dalí's '50 Secrets of Magical Craftsmanship', which he had conceived in California in 1945, was published in America. In it he offered in humorous vein the sum of his knowledge about perfection in painting. He called it *a kind of culinary initiation into the mysteries of painting*[134] in which the most widely varied themes were vividly stirred up together to form a medley of flavours. Pronouncements about the *secret of the painter's chaste and sensually-happy periods and the secret of a painter's marriage* [135] jostle with perspicacious pronouncements about draughtsmanship and painting, the properties of colours, mixing, preserving and drying paints, the use of white, the flexibility of artistic media, the quality of brushes, the magic of the spiral and the Golden Section.

The climax comes in the last lines: if a painter has now mastered and understood it all, *that alone is of absolutely no use [...]. For the final secret of this book is that at the moment when your hand is at your easel ready to paint, it must without question be guided by an angel.*[136] There is no success if 'fortune' does not smile on you.

Dalí was a phenomenon. Perhaps we all have a Dalí within us, just as we all have a child within us. If his spectacular actions had not found an echo in the latent rebellious stirrings of the good citizenry, he would certainly have had less effect.

Just as fairytales and myths do not recoil from images of cruelty and happy surprises, so Dalí dared to put before us the socially taboo. In so doing he was taking over the function assumed in so-called primitive societies by medicine men or shamans. He treated spiritual (or more frequently physical) impairment by conjuring up forces which are not accessible to socially correct members of the community. Just as the shamans transported themselves through their arts into a state of spectacular ecstasy – that is, a different form of consciousness – so he compelled 'sufferers' to confront forces they had refused to face.

If the post-modern mannerism of his paintings, with their emphasis on distortion, their infinite expanses and fragmentation, their double images and extrapolation into the bizarre and often the grotesque, had not belonged among fundamental channels for spiritual expression, he would have remained alone in his private world.

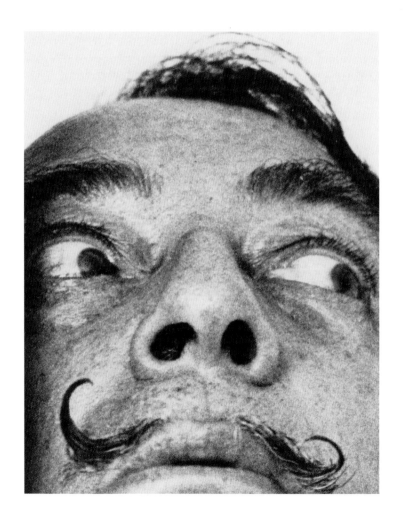

# New York - Paris - Port Lligat: Spanish renaissance (1948-1959)

When Dalí came home in July 1948, Spain had been a totalitarian state since the end of the Civil War. On 21 July he and Gala went straight from Le Havre to Port Lligat. *Only there am I at home; anywhere else I am just a visitor. This is not a feeling but a psychic, biological, surrealistic fact.*[137]

After all his successes in the 'vibrant' wider world of Paris and New York, the artist longed to find himself again in his own, familiar surroundings. *We live here in solitude and in the rhythm of the cosmic pulse. We fish for sardines by the light of the new moon, knowing that at the same time the lettuces are bolting instead of forming their hearts. We prefer to reflect on the genius of Paracelsus's inspiration rather than listen to the radio; we prefer to dream open-eyed about the invisible world, rather than let ourselves be seduced by television; we prefer to fly to the summit of the absolute rather than struggle for Utopian socialism. Like an industrious working man I look after my plot and my boat – that is, the picture I'm painting at the moment – and delight in simple things.*[138]

Dalí felt that he was tied not only to the familiar places of his childhood but also to Catholicism, his mother's religion, to which his free-thinking father had returned in old age. Was this sentimental nostalgia, a long-rejected yearning for the security of his childhood? It may partly have been opportunism, for under Franco the church was a political power. In any case on 23 November 1949 Dalí was received in private audience by Pope Pius XII, to whom he proudly presented his *Madonna of Port*

Dalí and Gala looling at The Madonna of Port Lligat

*Lligat* (1949; 48.9 x 37.5 cm), the first in a whole series of paintings on religious subjects.

In the 1950s both his life and his art were changing direction. Seeing that he had won his place among the financially powerful and culturally influential people of the western world, this man in his fifties had no longer any need to fear that his individuality would be submerged by the masses or manipulated by others if he did not resist them. Salvador Dalí had not come home as a prodigal son nor as a petitioner. He visited his father in his brand-new Cadillac and parked the car ostentatiously in front of the house. The notary no longer had any influence or power; he was just an old man retired from public life.

Dalí's sister Ana Maria had found a new way to hurt her brother, by publishing in Barcelona in 1949 a slim volume entitled *Salvador Dalí visto por su hermana (Salvador Dalí seen by his Sister)*. She described her brother's life in quite different terms than those he had used in his *Secret Life*. Ana Maria dressed up their childhood as an idyll and made her brother out as an ungrateful son who had wrongfully attacked his father, committed sacrilege and married a divorcée.

Dalí was furious about this destruction of the aura he had created around himself and reacted with a public 'justification': *In 1930 I was thrown out by my family without a penny. I am indebted for my international triumph solely to God's help, to the light of the Empordá and to the heroic daily sacrifice of an incomparable woman, my wife Gala.*[139]

In the previous decade Dalí's works had both moved the public and won their place in the world of international art and culture. Now he could challenge the masterpieces of the past with his own. In view of this, he could yield to his desire to be part of the history of art and expressed this in a reassessment of tradition. It would, however, be wrong to think that he was turning back out of remorse; he would not have been Dalí if he had not put his own, indelible imprint on traditional values. In 1951 he explained his purpose under the provocative title 'Mystical Manifesto, in which quantum physics and morphology are the central keywords'. *Form is the reaction of material to inquisitorial pressure on all sides from hard and relentless planes. Beauty is always the utmost spasm of a long, relentlessly severe, inquisitorial process. Freedom is formlessness. Every rose grows in a prison.*[140]

Like Goethe in the *Metamorphosis of Plants*, Dalí was looking for the formative principle behind the development of living things. 'Form' is not to be understood as a set of external dimensions, but as defining the principle which shapes every work of nature or art. The 'prison' to which he refers is the rose's formative principle; it cannot turn into either a washstand or a dahlia, because the potential for its development follows a blueprint, which governs the relationship of its parts to its whole.

Nietzsche's argument, that the compulsion to assume a clearly defined form overrides every other compulsion, could also apply to the blank surface of a canvas, because it is open to all possibilities.

In his 'Manifesto' Dalí posed the ultimate question of how to find a way to turn a nebulous idea into an incisive shape. Surrealist art was based on a sort of self-regulation, by which the principle underlying the dynamic of each work could be determined and developed, though without any conscious exertion of control over the process. From the 1950s on Dalí was looking for a different method. Without abandoning his vision of the paradox which defies reasonable interpretation, he now accepted and acknowledged the premise behind the realistic paintings of the High Renaissance as an authentic tradition, involving certain compositional techniques, such as the Golden Section and symmetry and, more importantly, the expressive gestures of mannerist painting.

Dalí and Gala at Port Lligat

This new orientation gave Dalí a wider range of themes, such as birth, love and death as depicted in the classical tradition of Christian religious paintings based on biblical stories – the Madonna, the Crucifixion, martyrdom, the Resurrection and the Last Supper. To these he added themes from Greek mythology and classical literature and violently rejected his contemporaries' recourse to *more or less barbaric artistic periods.*[141] He wanted nothing to do with abstract painters, either.

In his own way, Dalí was tending towards atomic physics as his models. While Freud had shown that the spiritual element was not formed by the schoolroom psychology jingle of 'thinking/feeling/wanting', this new concept of the material element had revealed that it existed not in the dimensions of time and space, but in a weightless, dynamic relationship between forces. By the time he painted *The Madonna of Port Lligat,* he was no longer firmly setting solid objects on a surface; everything seemed to be floating in the air as though it could take on a new shape at any moment, in spite of over-all strongly symmetrical constructions. *Since the theory of relativity replaced the substratum of the universe with the ether, deposed time and returned it to its relative role, [...] since the whole universe seems to be filled with this unknown and illusory substance and since the equilibrium of mass-energy exploded, everyone who thinks beyond the intransigence of Marxism knows that metaphysicians have to work with precision on the question of 'substance'.*[142]

Dalí was always a thinking painter. His surrealist pictures of the 1930s were no slick reproductions of a casual vision but inventions which he realised in a waking state and developed into vehicles of symbolic meaning, cleverly contriving 'illusory' objects such as soft watches, burning giraffes or elephants with stilt-like legs. From the 1950s on his programme was to construct and plan his pictures (at least his oils) according to certain principles. A mathematician may even have worked with him on the exact arrangement of the sections of his *Leda Atomica* (1949; 61.10 x 45.30 cm).

His Spanish contemporaries were painting quite differently. Tapies, Saura and Millares had discovered for themselves an informal style, not organising or planning their pictures but relying on formlessness and the inclusion of simple materials such as sackcloth, string, earth and wood to convey their meaning. The result was a sort of 'substance surrealism', while Dalí was contemplating the *Instability of Material* and *Nuclear Mysticism,* through which he hoped *to be able to communicate the great new cosmogony of our era.*[143]

In America the moderns were also heading in a different direction, witness the abstract expressionism of the Hofmann school, the works of Robert Motherwell (who concentrated on the effect of colour in space) and the action-painting or 'dripping' of Jackson Pollock, whose paint dribbled or spattered in its own way across the canvas. The effect of using differing materials and ways of expression to create form posed a new challenge to figurative drawing.

Only when Dalí was working with ink or watercolour, or was making prints or lithographs, did he allow himself a similar kind of formal freedom. The idea of introducing an element of chance (like the 'aleatory' principle in musical performance) is present in Dalí's illustrations. His style was therefore drifting in two different directions, according to his choice of medium.

On his return to Spain Dalí did not suffer from the iron rule of Franco's dictatorial regime; he could come and go at will, because from the middle of the 1950s Spain was trying to present a new face to the world, particularly as regards its artists, who were encouraged to act as its representatives abroad. He did, however, finally lose the sympathy of his Communist comrades. Buñuel

Leda Atomica, 1949 (oil on canvas)

had turned his back on Spain and was having to make his films in the most stringent financial conditions in Mexico, where he was constantly fighting against censorship.

Gala and Salvador were very happy living among the super-rich and famous. In 1951 they went to Venice, where Charles de Béstegui had invited them to a fancy-dress ball at the Palazzo Labia. They appeared as seven-metre high giants in costumes by Dior, who was also among the guests. Everyone was eccentrically dressed, so that it would have been easy to be overlooked – but not if dressed as giants!

Dalí's life had taken on a rhythm of working in his Port Lligat retreat and travelling. Lectures to publicise his current aesthetic theory and exhibitions and sales of his works took him to major cities. He and Gala often went to Paris and usually spent the winter months in the USA. There was no comparable market open to his works in Spain, although in 1953 through economic aid from the USA (in return for military defence bases), as well as through the budding tourist industry, the economy did begin to revive after its downturn due to the Civil War. However, Spanish society and culture were still not orientated towards the modern life of Paris, London, Rome or New York.

Dalí's art was becoming more and more an American phenomenon. In the Carstairs Gallery and later the Knoedler in New York both old and new works were regularly exhibited. From 7 to 18 February 1952 he undertook a lecture tour through seven states to debate his nuclear mysticism and atomic art and also made a point of attacking socialist realism. In March 1954 his 102 watercolour illustrations for Dante's *Divine Comedy* were exhibited in Rome, together with 41 oils from all his stylistic periods. The exhibition travelled to Milan and Venice and made for him a lasting name in Italy.

Aside from his other projects, he had been working on the *Divine Comedy*[144] for nearly ten years on a commission from the

Italian government for the poet's 700th anniversary. By a costly, complex process the watercolours were later turned into coloured woodcuts which could be printed in a large format. The result of this intensive piece of work was one of the most important sets of illustrations of the 20th century. Together with Picasso and Max Ernst he counts among the most influential of modern illustrators.

The fantastic element in reality was not just Dalí's subject but his artistic method as well. He was also an innovator in graphic printing, which from the middle of the 1970s made him by far the most popular and best-selling artist of the 20th century – and brought him a great deal of envy and criticism. 'Dalí's graphic creations were characterised by their careful and costly preparation. He corrected and altered the designs and elaborated and accentuated the needle's imprint on the plate – in short, he was involved throughout the production process. And he engaged the best engravers of our time [...].' [145]

Dalí wrote: *For thirty years Dante, condemned to death and living in exile, dreamt of Beatrice whom he had only met once in passing. He sought refuge in his vision: 'It was granted to me' he wrote, 'to gaze on a wonderful apparition, in whom I saw something which moved me not to speak more of this blessed creature until I was able to express myself with greater skill. To attain that goal I am working as hard as I can, which in truth she knows.'* [146] He then quoted the final words of the poem, which were to him the key to it: *'The love which moves the sun and the other stars.' The love which enabled him to remain alive and the stars where he hoped to find Beatrice again. I imagined myself without Gala and felt a crushing fear [...].* [147]

Dalí was developing his own kind of 'tachism', as we see even more clearly in his illustrations for Cervantes's *Don Quixote* than in his watercolours for Dante. The technique of applying flecks of paint – 'taches' - he here raised to the level of a pictorial medium.

In 1956 the French publisher Joseph Forêt brought him some lithographic stones, but Dalí did not want to have anything to do with lithography, because he considered it *without strength, without monarchy, without Inquisition.*[148] He suggested firing ink at the stones and his friend Georges Mathieu, a French representative of this school of art, gave him a *marvellous arquebus* (a 15th-century firearm). *The great event took place on 26 November 1956 on a barge on the Seine where, surrounded by a hundred sheep, I fired a bullet dipped in lithographic ink onto the stone, thus producing a wonderful spray effect. For a moment I recognised an angelic flight of perfect dynamic which represented the summit of achievement, and so I invented 'bulletism'.*[149] He then celebrated his new method in New York, where in the military academy every morning he fired at a lithographic stone, which immediately turned it into a rain of dollars!

Dalí shooting a litho stone

Of course this was not enough for Dalí; he had to carry the experiment further, by designing a 24-kilo bronze bas relief. Unlike with his oil paintings, he put his thoughts about this enterprise in writing: *I started in apocalyptic exaltation to hack up the block of wax with an axe. I worked in the open air at a table on the beach at Port Lligat. I stuck a cake of honey into the wax, because honey is always the symbol of holiness in the Old Testament, and I put in golden needles to make an aureole around Christ, with on it an agate as a symbol of purity. […] Finally I added a knife and fork as symbols of everyday life […].*[150]

Next time he created the illustrations with the help of a bomb which he exploded in the old winter cycle track in Paris. He fixed a watch, medals and nails to the explosive device and fired it all onto a copper plate. Above this motif he drew a *pietà* and painted it in watercolours.[151]

Meanwhile he was giving lectures, always with some sort of visual effect. In December 1955 he was driven by a chauffeur in a black and white Rolls Royce filled with cauliflowers to the Sorbonne, where he gave an address on 'Phenomenological Aspects of the Paranoiac-Critical Method 'to frenzied applause. He chose as his example Vermeer's *Lacemaker* in which, by rearranging its structure, he claimed to have discovered the logarithmic curves of rhinoceros horns, which became a new Dalinian yardstick for judging and constructing his pictures.

The conflict with his family rumbled on. In 1954 he painted *Young Girl auto-sodomized by the Horns of her own Chastity* [152] – an aggressively erotic back view of a nude, her curvaceous upper torso leaning out of a window, with her body dismembered or held together with outsize phallic rhinoceros horns. It is a reworking of his *Girl standing at the Window* from 1925, for which Ana Maria, fully dressed, had modelled for her student brother.

In his 'nuclear' paintings Dalí developed an idiosyncratic kind of neo-cubism. He chopped up solid physical things into particles, which he then arranged in dynamic turns and twists, waves, ellipses, whirls, swathes and spirals, so that they blended together

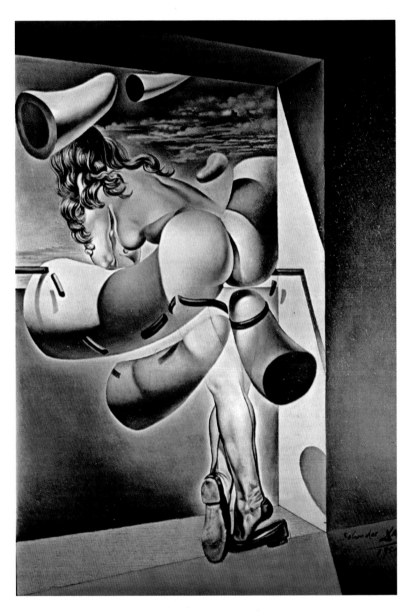

Young Virgin auto-sodomised by the Horns of her own Chastity, 1954

Lacemaker and Rhino

into heads or bodies, while leaving spaces between them. The objects and even the atoms were not single entities but products of a tense relationship between forces beyond normal perception. This was a lesson in how to look at things, which he had learnt from atomic physics. It is up to the viewer to relate these images either to space and lightness or to catastrophic destruction caused by an explosion.

From the 1950s on Dalí often chose as his models historical works such as Raphael's *Sistine Madonna*, Vermeer's *Lacemaker* or figures from Michelangelo or Velázquez. This is certainly not a ruse by someone who has run out of ideas after 30 years of work. No painter is obliged to create his visions of the world around him out of nothing or out of his private spiritual world. Painting is a world in itself, in which interaction can take place between works from any age.

Dalí elaborated on old pictures and on his own, for example, on what was possibly his most hallucinatory painting *The Persistence of Memory*.[153] The watch – the exact measuring instrument which enables us to grasp the chronology of what we call the passage of 'time' – he has transformed into something like melting camembert, so pliable that it can drape itself over the branch of a leafless tree, the edge of a platform or a surreal invention which is often unthinkingly called the great masturbator. The face, hands and winder are those of a pocket watch. Time, the great theme of Martin Heidegger and other existential philosophers, is here given – or perhaps given back – another quality than that of chronology. The pocket watch has become the expression of a mysterious spiritual state – creeping, brooding or clinging. There is a breathless quality about the picture. The light on the plain, sky and objects suggests the transition from day to night or from night to morning – an atmosphere which belongs to neither dreams nor wakefulness, rising nor sinking. It is somehow in limbo, arrested, neither living nor dead, reminiscent of Henri Bergson's 'durée' (a concept of time as one indivisible span)[154] or 'bardo' – the Buddhists' transitional state between life and death.[155] *The Persistence of Memory* shares this quality with a large group of Dalí's paintings of the 1930s and 1940s.

The revised picture *The Disintegration of the Persistence of Memory* (1952-54; 25 x 33 cm) creates a different effect. The softness of the watches is now disagreeably contrasted with the hard, rectangular precision of small bricks, so arranged that the

The Persistence of Memory, 1931 (oil on canvas).
Museum of Modern Art, New York, USA

flat plain is covered with the pattern created by them and the spaces between them. The relentless regularity of geometrical detailing conflicts with historicity and the nostalgia of memory. The expanse of the sea is not on a normal, uniform level but rises at one end like a piece of skin. The tree is broken up into pieces. Bullets are firing over the shore as though aiming at a variety of objects; they throw one of the watches into the air and penetrate the body of a great fish. Do not disturb the sleep of the world ...

In 1952 both the artist's father and Paul Éluard died. Dalí did not attend either funeral; for him nothing existed but his work. At the age of 50 he was embarking on a regular frenzy of new projects and whereas for a long while his paintings had been very small,[156] from then on they were enormous.

Like the old masters Dalí engaged an assistant, the stage designer Isidor Bea, who for the next 30 years helped him with technical problems, firstly for *The Last Supper* (1955; 167 x 268 cm). A geometrical construction in the centre indicating a window allows the darkened interior to blend into the translucent colours of sea, mountains and sky outside. Christ seems to be rising out of the sea with a small fishing boat in front of his breast. While the apostles are arranged singly around a large table, bowed down in prayer, Christ appears full-face, his bearing symbolic and expressive. He is looking slightly upwards towards where a disproportionately large torso with arms seems to be rising into the heavens. Religious legend and concrete naturalism are here inseparable, reminiscent of Goethe's saying: 'nothing is within, nothing is without, for what is within is also without'. Chester Dale, a collector of French impressionists, bought *The Last Supper* and gave it to the National Gallery of Art in Washington.

Dalí's next painting was *The Sistine Madonna* (also known as *Ear with Madonna*), another typical large-scale work (1958; 223

Dalí in the garden of his house in Port Lligat, 1957.

x 190 cm). 'Seen close to, this is an abstract picture almost entirely painted in grey, but from two metres away it turns into Raphael's *Sistine Madonna* and from 15 metres looks like ear of an angel, a metre and a half across.'[157] A film seems to cover the whole surface, like a greatly enlarged newspaper photograph. This technique became fashionable in the 1960s and can be found in other forms in the paintings of the German Sigmar Polke, but Dalí was the first and the best at using it.[158]

In 1958 Salvador and Gala renewed their marriage vows in private and without display in a Catholic ceremony in the church of Saint Marti Vell near Girona. In a private audience with Pope John XXIII Salvador told him of his plan to build a floating cathedral in the Arizona desert, in which all Christian religions would be united under one roof.

# On top of his world:
## between pop art and pomp art
## (1960-1969)

*As befitted my fame, my sales and the importance of my art and my
ideas, I was one of the kings of the world. The dollars never ceased to
rain down on me.*[159]

By the 1960s running the Dalí enterprise had become too
much for Gala and at the beginning of 1960 Salvador engaged as
his business manager an Irish army captain John Peter Moore,
who was director of European intelligence for London Films
International and a member of the propaganda department of
the Vatican (he is said to have arranged for Dalí an audience with
the Pope at 24 hours' notice). Moore was entitled to ten percent
of his own sales of Dalí merchandise, which in the course of the
next years comprised shirts, fabrics, ties, cognac bottles, calen-
dars, ashtrays for Air India, stamps for Guyana, bathing costumes and gilt oyster knives. 'Hundreds of people are working
round the clock on Dalí products' reported *Life* magazine. In the
Aubusson factory several dozen women were busily weaving gold
threads into tapestries designed by Dalí, some 30 glass-blowers in
Nancy were kept busy making glass heads and plates and else-
where 30 more men were producing the same things in bronze. A
handful of master jewellers was creating flower-like pieces and
other small, exquisite and expensive objects designed by the master.[160] Within a few years his ten percent had made Moore a
multi-millionaire.

Dalí's American collectors Reynolds and Eleanor Morse were
not pleased to see their artistic genius descending into the

mundane world of commerce. They feared that Dalí's paintings might appear in a bad light as a result but quite the opposite happened. If ordinary people could not afford to buy his works, they could at least acquire an artefact or one of his large-edition graphics, which would give them something from the hand of the well-publicised crazy genius.

Gala gathered around her a number of younger men who interested her both sexually and maternally. In the early Port Lligat years she had enjoyed the company of the muscular young fishermen and she frequently went on the prowl, particularly in Paris and New York. For years she pampered William Rotlein, a homeless heroin addict whom she had picked up in Brooklyn. He was 40 years younger than her, stole from her regularly and deluded himself that she would leave Salvador and marry him. Gala took him to Rome, Florence, Turin and Verona – where she fantasised about the two of them as a freakish Romeo and Juliet – and finally, suddenly, put him onto a transatlantic flight (in first-class), after the Italian tabloid press had published a report with a

Dalí and Amanda Lear

photograph about the 'unusual love affair between the grandmother and the lad' and the 'lad' was preparing to tell the whole world about his relationship with Gala. [161]

For his part Salvador surrounded himself with young men and women of the international set, mostly in Gala's absence. Since 1955 he had been seen in public escorting Nanita Kalachnikoff and in 1965 he became fascinated by Amanda Lear, a transsexual who had been called Alain Tap and after her operation worked as a model and pop-singer. Moore could arrange contacts with all possible kinds of people and part of his job was to find Dalí collaborators for his erotic scenarios. 'Dalí's "erotic masses" ceased to be secret affairs, because in the sexually liberated atmosphere of the 1960s he could allow the wings of his fantasies to spread themselves. He rented palaces and filled them with dwarves and transvestites, trapeze artists and ocelots.' [162] He also indulged himself as a masturbating voyeur of the sexual activities of others.

Ludmilla Tcherina, dancing the Woman (Gala)

In public Gala was the object of Dalí's whole love and respect; she often appeared in his pictures, frequently as Our Lady, which upset many people. In fact he was following in the footsteps of the Renaissance artists who often used their wives or mistresses as models for the Madonna. This situation seemed unaffected by the fact that in their everyday lives they quarrelled and screamed at each other like cat and dog. The Gala of the paintings embodied a complex figure made up of muse, mother, femme fatale, angel and tutelary goddess.

The premiere of the *Le Ballet de Gala* took place in Venice in August 1961. This was a new ballet by Pierre Rhallys and Maurice Béjart to music by Scarlatti, for which Dalí designed and Isidor Bea built five fantastic sets measuring nine by seven metres. Ludmilla Tcherina, who danced the Woman (Gala), 'launched into some of the most erotic dancing …', wrote

Dalí in Castor and Pollux helmet

*Time*, 'in a black leotard so tight that she seemed more nude than nude'.[163]

Dalí was as usual warring against contemporary artistic trends. In his eyes neo-dada style was producing wretched imitations of Duchamp's 'ready-mades' and other dadaist and surrealist products, some of which, including the *Aphrodisiac Jacket*, he had made himself some 30 years earlier.

Every period has its art and every art its period. In the 1960s it became clear that the ubiquitous slogans and images reminiscent of baroque church architecture used in advertising had, almost unnoticed, turned practical things and consumer goods into fetishes or quasi-religious votive objects. Pop art brought this out so forcefully that it turned the banal into a conspicuous object of adoration. Banality was beginning to evolve.

Having declared that Renaissance painting was the future, Dalí was now extolling the battle-pictures of the Catalan Mariano Fortuny and the Frenchman Ernest Meissonier and through them the despised genre of historical paintings (the pop art of the 19th century). In Fortuny's *Battle of Tetuan* he said he could see *virtuosity through regular stains*.[164] He painted his revised versions of the academic art of 'pompierism' (from the French term for uninspired, conventional art) in this manner, thereby producing something his enemies called kitsch but he called *Dalí's pop art*. It could even be called 'pomp art'. In the 1970s he painted the walls and ceilings of his houses in an exaggerated version of this style, though not without a tinge of irony.

Beside the thinker-painter and the paranoiac-critical visionary, who created authentic faces in hyper-realistic manner to make one think everything was just an illusion, including what the realists claimed as 'real', there was yet another painter lurking within Dalí – the joker. The humour and irony we enjoy in his writings are also there in his paintings. By his affectations of greatness and deep emotion he may have created the impression that he took everything deadly seriously, but his didactic manner disguised the fact that he was having fun at the expense of the world.

His huge pictures (from the 1960s on they measured up to three by four metres) were working towards raising the barriers between kitsch and art, which has been a continual subject for vehement debate. The American author and literary critic Susan Sontag did kitsch a great service and gave it a new cachet in the 1960s by christening it 'camp'.[165] The perverted idealisation of the banal behind the products of kitsch can, once we have acknowledged its existence, open up a special kind of experience, provided we are not suffocated by its sugary over-sentimentality. Everyone exaggerates, beautifies and idealises and in the casualties among kitsch products we can detect and observe this tendency. It is not the object itself, but the effect it has on us, which determines whether it is art or kitsch. If objectively studying something dismissed as kitsch

'If you understand your painting in advance, you might just as well not paint it at all.' (Dalí: *50 Magical Secrets of Craftsmanship*)

leads to a personal experience of spiritual self-knowledge, the barrier between art and kitsch has been raised.

This applied to Dalí's new kitsch art. All the histrionics, the caricaturing and the games he played with this jumble make it look as though he is treating classical iconography in the same way as pop art treated its discovery of the original iconography of the new media.

Hardly anything is more suited to moving seamlessly between kitsch, pomp and art than the theatre. Negotiations with the Mayor of Figueres, Ramon Guardiola Rovira, who wanted some Dalí works for the town's Empordá Museum, finally led to a project to rebuild the town's theatre, which had been destroyed in the Civil War, as a museum – just for Dalí. 'Finished in 1850, the Teatro Principal in Figueres was on the lavish scale befitting a garrison town. [...] When Dalí was a child it was the only theatre in Figueres, and it was here that he saw his first plays. [...] in the theatre's foyer, now a heap of blackened stones, he had first exhibited his work.' [166]

On 12 August 1960 a bullfight and other celebrations were held in honour of the 56-year-old Dalí, who drove round the bullring in his Cadillac. Jutting out of the top of the convertible was one of the giant figures from Béstegui's masked ball. At the end of the fiesta a plaster steer filled with firecrackers was set off (no Spanish folk festival would be complete without fireworks). The town also honoured its famous son by affixing a commemorative plaque to the façade of the house where he was born.

Dalí is said to have remarked that his *Battle of Tetuan* (1962; 308 x 406 cm) was the largest piece of kitsch he had ever painted. It was his ironic commentary, opulent and accomplished, on the conquest by Spain of the Moroccan city of Tetuan in 1860 and was exhibited beside Fortuny's unfinished original (300 x 972 cm), which Dalí's work exceeded in size by several square metres. Whether it was kitsch, irony or a painter's self-indulgence, the American millionaire Huntingdon Hartford bought it for his Gallery of Modern Art in New York. He had already commissioned from Dalí *The Discovery of America by Christopher Columbus* (1958-59; 410 x 284 cm), a work with interesting op art characteristics. The expanses of sky and the celestial groups in many of Dalí's large pictures remind one of the 19th-century English painter, John Martin - in particular *The Ecumenical Council* and a work with the unpronounceable name *Galacidalacideoxyribononucleicacid* (1963; 305 x 345 cm), subtitled *Homage to Crick and Watson,* the discoverers of DNA. Since 1953 the molecules which contain the genetic code of every living cell were frequently to be found in Dalí's works in formal, rhythmic patterns which extrapolate the organic forms into an abstract code.

Dalí's large-scale works are often slated or sniped at by art critics, some of whom one suspects of prejudging them. To reach the inner meaning of a picture one has to absorb oneself in it, for instance *The Station of Perpignan* (1965; 295 x 406 cm) in the Museum Ludwig in Cologne.

In the middle of this picture is a bright rectangle on which one's eye immediately focuses and from which light orange beams shine into the four corners of the canvas. From bright rectangle, a human figure with outstretched arms and slightly bent legs is leaping out, either towards the viewer or towards the female figure with her back turned. Her hair is like Gala's and she crouches in the exact centre of the bottom of the picture, on a bag resting on a Millet-style cart, which stands at the edge of a sea in the sky. In the four sections between the beams are murky, vague, misty objects taken from Millet's *Angelus*. To the left is the man, praying humbly with bowed head but floating above a sack, to the right the woman, also humbly praying and also floating above a sack with a pitchfork in front of her. To the left a wheelbarrow is being loaded with sacks by a man and a woman – once

The Station of Perpignan, 1965.
Museum Ludwig, Cologne, Germany

again vague, as though in a mist – she is on the right, bending forward to pick up a sack, while he is in the act of taking her from behind – but this is again just vaguely suggested.

Above the bright rectangle is a railway truck and above it another man, larger than the one in the middle but in the same attitude, leaping towards us. This whole scene is set in the sky. A single, well-defined wooden shoe is floating in the lower section and on it is a diagonal, blood-red slash – the stigmata. Like a mirage, as though it were painted on a different plane, a crown of thorns appears above the bright rectangle. Only gradually does one distinguish a head and, under the diagonal shafts of light, outstretched arms – images of the crucified Christ. With a trick of perspective the diagonal beams of light consign the central, glowing rectangle deep into the background, yet the effect of its bright colour is to draw it simultaneously forward, so that the centre springs out at us as the man does. Unlike many of Dalí's other large-scale paintings cluttered with detail, this picture contains wide, empty expanses of background colour.

The centre of the space shifts backwards and forwards, floating, falling, climbing; the space itself is moving, while the figures in the four sections between the beams of light are in a state of trance-like rigidity. The railway truck above the head with the crown of thorns would seem to be an irrelevance if the painting were not called *The Station of Perpignan.* It suggests waiting for movement through space, journeying, recalling troubles and weariness and also anticipating ease of movement. It is a combination of solid construction and a feeling of hazy, dream-like falling or flying. [167]

Dalí explained: *I had a kind of cosmic energy [...]. About the station I could see a radiating aura in a perfect circle: the metal trolley cables of the streetcars that ringed the edifice and gave it a crown of glinting light. [...] The centre of the universe was there before me.*[168] The original title of the picture has a playfully ironic ring to it: *Gala looking at Dalí in a state of anti-gravitation in the work of art 'Pop-op-yes-pompier', in which one can contemplate the two 'anguishing' characters from Millet's Angelus in a state of atavistic hibernation [...].*[169]

In December 1965 the painting was exhibited in New York at the Knoedler Gallery, which thereafter presented Dalí's newest works every year. His sphere of influence had meanwhile extended far beyond Europe and the United States and in 1964 Japan had held a huge retrospective of 72 paintings and 63 other works in Tokyo, Nagoya and Kyoto.

Now in his sixties, the artist's life-style was as ever full of contrasts. In April 1964 he received the Grand Cross of Queen Isabella of Spain and in July gave an interview to *Playboy* magazine. In May

Signing books

1965 he designed a collection of bathing costumes with breasts on the back which was displayed in the Hotel Meurice in Paris. In December, he walked along Fifth Avenue dressed up as Father Christmas to sign copies of his *Diary of a Genius* at Doubleday's. In January 1966 he designed an envelope for the UN's invitations to the 20th anniversary of its foundation – and so it went on.

In December 1965 Huntington Hartford's Gallery of Modern Art in New York mounted a gigantic exhibition for Dalí: 170 paintings, 60 drawings, prints, plastic works and artefacts displayed on four floors. The curious, the art-lovers and the critics were divided into two camps, one preferring his small, surrealist works from the 1930s and dismissing the later ones, such as *Christ of St John of the Cross, The Apotheosis of the Dollar* or *The Discovery of America by Christopher Columbus.*

People had become accustomed to the earlier works. Surrealism had suffered the same fate as all artistic movements which are originally revolutionary and avant-garde, in that once accepted by the museums and absorbed into the canon of culture, it had lost its bite and been tamed like a wild animal in a zoo. It inspired neither horror nor a desire to run away. Sanctioned as it was by society's institutions, people had learnt to find it 'interesting' and eventually even 'beautiful', or at least 'beautifully crazy'. The pictures were no longer shocking.

On the other hand the new works Dalí had painted since declaring his mystical conversion aroused rage and irritation, and he was reproached for betraying surrealism and himself in the pursuit of wealth. It was repeatedly said that he had reverted to realism (referring to his own countless quotations from his early works) and just wanted to make an impression; also that his painting technique looked like Italian calendar art and had the artistic quality of a chocolate box. The critic Carlton Lake was also upset by 'the obtrusive make-up man's technique: the highlights and glints. It was the Hard Sell made flesh.'[170] Others saw in Dalí's large-scale pictures (18 in all) a step in the direction of modern classicism. One representative of this school of thought was Reynolds Morse, who provided many exhibits from his own collection. To him the new paintings were 'masterpieces'. While the purism which governed the views of both camps did not do justice to the originality of the works produced after the end of the 1950s, in the 21st century a new perspective is emerging. While Dalí's early surrealist paintings demonstrated his revolt against modernism, the later works expressed a kind of post-modern, eclectic attitude. He was more culturally knowledgeable than most artists and, among other things, familiar with the great masterpieces of European literature. There was hardly a work among them which he had not illustrated.

Dalí 'plundered' images from cultural and art history and used them cavalierly as though they were a treasure trove. He adopted, and frequently reconstructed with dramatic irony, religious themes (the Crucifixion, the Madonna or the sufferings of the saints), scientific discoveries (atomic physics, genetics and holography), current events (the dropping of the atomic bomb, the Ecumenical Council, the worship of money or advertising), historical events (the conquest of America or the Battle of Tetuan) and figures from classical and local legend (Venus, Daphne, the Judgment of Paris, Hercules, tuna-fishing and bullfights). As in post-modernist architecture, his post-surrealist paintings contained a pluralistic sign language which purported to be historical and he invented a new system for decoding it in each painting. He chose the most varied methods of painting, juxtaposing pop-art and op-art techniques with neo-cubist decomposition, photographically realistic illusions with basic patterns, romantic landscape-painting with surrealistically, exaggeratedly designed sequences, psychedelic intimations with dot-matrix surfaces, tachism with geometric abstraction and action painting with pointillism.

Not only his large-scale works underwent a long period of gestation with many interim drafts, but in the ones measuring many square metres one can easily follow the progression from small-scale sketches through pencil, ink or water-colour studies of standing youths or women and through the structural plans for the large surfaces. These were staging posts from a small format through a large one to the completed work. After basic preparation, the full-size canvas often started mistily with the thinnest layers of paint and only gradually developed into its final, incisive form.

So it is with the process of creating *Tuna Fishing* (1966-67; 304 x 404 cm). The scene is highly dramatic and depicts a whole universe. It took Dalí two summers to paint. Behind the welcome arrival of this nourishing fish on our market stalls lies a bloody struggle between hunter and prey. We see the wrestling, stabbing, striking and fighting at close quarters, the fish being overpowered in the spouting, whirling, blue-green water which is turning red with blood, or leaping away in flight. The colours of the men's bodies are broken up into patterns, as though designed by a computer. The agonised expressions and bearing of two of the figures (of which he borrowed one from mannerist, over-proportioned Greek sculpture) speak of the death and dying of human beings as well as fish. This painting was first exhibited in November 1967 in the 'Homage to Meissonier' exhibition in the Hotel Meurice in Paris. *Dalí's father had told him about tuna fishing when he was a child. Besides, he showed him a print of tuna fishing by a Swiss artist (a 'pompier') [...].* [171]

If one expects deeply meaningful theorising from Dalí, one

will find banality, and vice versa. The design for the dust-jacket of *Dalí de Draeger* (1968) came to him while walking past the publisher's showcase: '[…] as Dalí suddenly stopped, took a few steps back and pointed to the packaging of a cassette ornamented with the arms of the Marquise de Sévigny, he shouted: *There! That's what the cover of our book should look like!* At a single glance he had invented the most surrealist and fashionable of all dust-jackets.'

Painting a horse

172 The 'edible beauty' of the artist's works presented in the book in detailed enlargements turned into a chocolate box lid! He did not care about the critics' accusations that his pictures were kitsch; he picked up the word and from then on spoke about his new *kitsch art* (pompierism).

In this book, which immediately went through six editions and made the author, the publisher Charles Draeger and Captain Moore all a little richer, Dalí arranged his works not chronologically but under themes – *War, Landscape, Gala, Still-life, the Erotic, Mysticism, Space-Time* and *Oneiros* (Dream). Its interest lay in the mixture of black-and-white and colour reproductions of enlarged details and complete pictures. Draeger annotated it with forthright comments on Salvador Dalí's art and life.

Dalí diagnosed himself lucidly in the final chapter: *I am a polymorph, an inveterate and anarchic pervert. […] Everything affects me and nothing can alter me. I am effeminate, cowardly and repellent. My spirit had to reveal by the power of Spanish thinking the ultimate form of cruel, Jesuitical and implacable agate which is my strange genius. My parents christened me Salvador, and as the name says, I am destined for nothing less than to save painting from the emptiness of modern art in this age of catastrophes, in this mechanised and mediocre universe, in which we have the misfortune and the honour to live.* 173

Dalí was one of those people who are convinced they have a destiny (though he sometimes needed to talk himself into it). He was obsessed with proving this in his works and making everyone else see it, but he always had the courage to lay himself open to the judgment of others. As he sought to do justice to his calling, he claimed the right to follow maxims he had formulated for himself. Dalí certainly did not subscribe to what is today called 'political correctness' – on the contrary, many people disapproved of his posing as exceptional and it perplexed well brought-up, respectable citizens that he cared little about showing himself in a favourable light so that everyone would love him. From the end of the 1960s Dalí felt comfortable in the company of hippies – mostly young people who hoped for some advantage from being with him and some of whom posed for him as models. He surrounded himself with this entourage like a pop star. He was particularly taken with a certain Carlos Lozano, for whom he

'The only difference between me and a madman is that I am not mad.'
Dalí, 1934

managed to get a part in the musical 'Hair', and Amanda Lear was also an important part of his life. She appeared increasingly often at his side, including at a dinner given by Draeger at the Lido in Paris in 1968.

As a married couple the Dalís created intervals in their lives together, which they each filled with their own circle of admirers – in Gala's case of lovers, to the delight of the gossip columnists. In 1984 Amanda Lear published a book describing this scenario – credibly or not – called *Le Dalí d'Amanda*. [174] Enric Sabater Bonay, the publisher of the Girona newspaper *Los Sitios*, interviewed Dalí in 1968 and soon became his attendant spirit, photographing and reporting regularly on his activities. He also found for Gala the summer home she had long wanted – a derelict mansion in the nearby village of Púbol. [175] They had it thoroughly restored and Dalí decorated it with his new kitsch art. This was Gala's domain, which Salvador only entered with her permission.

Among Dalí's large-scale pictures *The Hallucinogenic Toreador* (1968-70; 398.8 x 299.7 cm) marked a kind of 'summa' or apotheosis of all his painting. In an arena of death and life he has collected every kind of object: Gala, angels, cliffs, the Venus de Milo, flies, fossils, landscape, a tear, corpuscles, cubism and a small boy with a hoop – in fact, references to the history of his paintings and his life. [176] In the torso of the Venus de Milo wrapped round an English box of Venus pencils Dalí had 'seen' a toreador which no one else had noticed.

In the middle of the picture, a parade of antique sculptures of Venus forms a triangle, which has its point at the left edge and spreads across to the right edge of the canvas. Venus in metamorphosis? Dolls from cultural history? A parade of mannequins? The two at the front in red and green robes are larger than life and the four figures turned away are smaller and fainter. Starting in the space between the two large figures one can discern the head of the toreador in Dalí's title, soft as though made of wax. Several heads of Venus float freely in space and, in the bottom right corner, somehow in another world with different dimensions, is a tiny boy in a sailor-suit with a hoop; in the top left corner, as far from him as possible, Gala's face appears as though imprinted on the legendary cloth which wiped away Christ's sweat, faint like a memory on a glowing, yellowish background.

The little boy stands in a landscape over which monstrously large flies with gigantic shadows are making towards him. The plain dissolves into a lake, on which float a minute figure of Venus and a tiny child lying on a mat (Moses?). In the lower left corner are two distorted, cubist figures of Venus. The hardly recognisable head of an ox rises out of the lake, morbidly decomposed and textured like marble; above it are small coloured balls (corpuscles?) and dark ovoid shapes with shadows, many of them winged, some of which also float over the expanse of the distant bullring at the top of the picture. The whole is vaulted over with the semicircular wall of the bullring with its tiers of seats, and tiny statues of Venus stand in the arches of the colonnade.

The outsize and the very small, the compact and the fragmented, the bright and the faint, triangle and circle, a minute world dominated by the powerful one of gods and myths, pictures within a picture (there is a double image with Voltaire's head in the red dress of the largest Venus) – this picture tells the story of human and cultural metamorphosis between birth and death.

In the image of the toreador who *because he is going to die, is already dead,* said Dalí, he is portraying his dead friends – García Lorca, René Crevel, the actor Pierre Batcheff (who appeared in *Un Chien Andalou*) and, last but not least, his dead brother, the prototype of his own life and death.[177] But before he came to die Dalí, together with his young admirers, created his own temple to ensure his survival after death – the Teatro-Museo (in Catalan: Teatre-Museu) Dalí in Figueres.

He was also pursuing his delight in painting ceilings, first for Gala's mansion and shortly afterwards for his museum.[178] Stereoscopic pictures were his newest interest and where did he find their source? In the old masters, of course. He was convinced that the painter Gérard Dou (a contemporary of Vermeer's) was his forerunner, saying that in one of Dou's paintings he could see a double image. He equipped himself with a Fresnel lens to create stereoscopic pictures and studied holography.[179]

He was far from exhausting all the potentials of painting. Almost as a sideline he completed some more advertising graphics, for instance a whole page for 'La Source Perrier', which appeared on 19 November 1969 in *France Soir* and three days later in *Paris Match*.

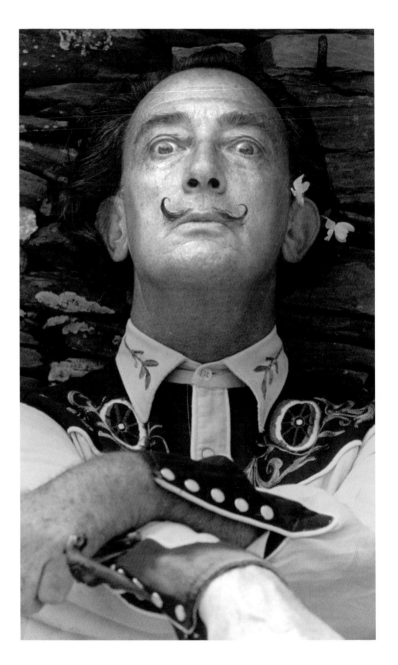

# The grand drama: living and dying in a total work of art (1970-1989)

On 10 October 1968 Dalí had another audience with General Franco, who approved a grant to finance the conversion of the Figueres theatre. In April 1970 an impatient Dalí gave a press conference in the Musée Gustave Moreau in Paris, to announce publicly the founding of the Dalí Museum. Two months later the Spanish cabinet decided to allocate the necessary funds and on 13 October work finally began. In emulation of the American architect Buckminster Fuller, inventor of the geodesic dome, Dalí designed for the roof a glass cupola (to him a symbol of monarchy),[180] and the Spanish architect Emilio Pérez Piñero constructed for him the dome which would become the symbol of the town of Figueres. He spent the next few years fitting out the Teatro-Museo but also found time to prepare more exhibitions,[181] illustrate books and design advertisements, receive honours, travel and embellish Gala's mansion.

As ever, he was finding his fulfilment through working. Sabater reported: 'Dalí was always at his easel by seven in the morning, and worked until lunchtime. Then came a siesta, then another work session. Only in the evening for a few hours would he relax. The pattern was invariable – with one exception: when Gala was about to go away on a jaunt with one of her lovers to Italy (her usual destination), Dalí would phone either Amanda or Nanita Kalachnikoff, who would arrive a few days later and stay for a week or two. Then and only then would Dalí give himself a break.'[182]

Dalí paid Amanda $60 an hour to model for him. She also occasionally helped him in his studio when Isidor Bea was not available and he gave her painting lessons. When he created the 1971 Special Christmas Number for the French edition of *Vogue* (the combined portrait of Mao Tse-tung and Marylin Monroe on the cover was to become famous) he honoured her with seven photographs, alongside many pages featuring Gala and Púbol.

Dalí's Museo is utterly different from the usual kind of museum in which spaces are kept neutral, so that the visitor's eye is not distracted from the paintings. This was more like the style of one of King Ludwig II of Bavaria's castles. (Dalí once said that everything in him was theatrical.) No building could have been more suitable than a theatre. The Teatro-Museo did not exhibit works, but became a work of art in itself – the greatest, accessible, 'total' work of art of Salvador Dalí. He himself designed the smallest details, from the loaves on the heads of the statues, the fully-dressed divers, the reliefs of bread on the façade and the monumental eggs on the roof, to the toilets and the poster for the state lottery inside.[183]

Dalí's works are distributed, untitled, around the whole building. There are paintings, stereoscopic photographs, a bendable metal crucifix, the *Rainy Taxi*, a room made out of a head of Mae West you can walk into, classical studies and also works by other artists like Bouguereau, Fortuny, Arno Breker, Ernst Fuchs, Wolf Vostell, Ramón Pitxot and Marcel Duchamp.[184] Many people look at the classical-style ceiling and wall paintings in bewilderment and perhaps even horror. The museum combines art, kitsch and caricature in confusingly ostentatious harmony.

In a programme for London Weekend Television Dalí said that his whole ambition for the Museo was to reconstruct his youth in Figueres and Cadaqués with all his early memories and erotic dreams. He was working high up on a ceiling painting when they were filming and from his scaffolding explained that the crutch on which he was working was a symbol of impotence. *Yes, all le great people who realise sensational achievements is impotent. Napoleon, everybody. Le people who is not impotent make childs, embrions, and no more. But immediately que le sex work with extreme difficulty, you create fantastic music, architecture and invasions – imperial invasions* (sic).[185]

There is no doubt that Dalí was talking about himself. Sublimation and perversion were the sources of his creative power. He used the bodies of young people to act out what he could not live out himself. As a result of the sexual revolution of the 1970s there were always plenty of them at his disposal, ready and willing to participate in his games. He was a curious mixture of detachment (he could not bear being touched) and sexually induced intimacy as a spectator. Dalí the voyeur was aroused and inspired by the writhing mix of bodies before his eyes and most strongly so when they were sodomising. Watching anal intercourse gave him the most intense sensations. As a follower of de Sade he had no inhibition in giving the epithet 'divine' to this ecstasy which he complemented by masturbating.

Dalí was certainly not one of those 'nice' people one would recommend to one's children or grandchildren as models, but more a copybook example of Gottfried Benn's thesis that art grows 'in the soil of paradox'. 'Among the 150 geniuses of the western world there are 50 homoerotics and perverts and droves of drug-addicts. [...] productiveness, wherever one comes across it, is permeated with anomalies, stigmatisation and paroxysms.' [186] What distinguished Dalí from many of the others was his urge to show off flamboyantly the source of his inspiration.

Looking at the contorted malleability, distortion and deformity in many of his pictures (not only in the pornographic drawings) often makes one uneasy. His whole oeuvre contains disturbing shifts between an urge towards the banal and highly stylised mannerist compositions. The images he invented in his earlier periods – floppy watches, burning giraffes, elephants on stilts, the profile of *The Great Masturbator*, Gala again and again, early stage designs, a large-scale print of *The Hallucinogenic Toreador* and much more – are an integral part of the artistic synthesis which is the Museo. There is also a quantity of sculptures scattered through the rooms. Dalí did not only make sculptures for 'surreal objects'; for years he had been producing plastic works in bronze and other materials. In the Museo hangs a *Contorted Christ* made of artificial material which he moulded in wax in miniature, like the ones he had made with his mother as a child. In his garden in Port Lligat lies an outsize *Christ* made of large pieces of junk, including an old boat. He made a bronze cast of Michelangelo's 'Slave', put it in a bronze tyre and called it *Michelin's Slave – Can be used as a Car* (1965); there are busts of Dante with spoons replacing laurels, of Velazquez with colourful little pop-art figures stuck in his face and of White Eagle.[187] The chairs, sofas, beds, chests and mirrors in the museum's rooms degenerate into bizarre sculptures.

On the upper floor there is a room reserved for exhibiting works by Catalan artists, including some by Antoni Pitxot, the nephew of the impressionist painter Dalí had admired in his youth. Pitxot created a world out of stones from the beach at Es Sortell in the manner of Arcimboldo.

In May 1974, having just returned from a Knoedler exhibition of his holographs in New York, Dalí had more discussion in Madrid with Franco and Prince Juan Carlos about a date for the opening of the Museum. In June he had a hernia operation but recovered quickly. The Teatro-Museo Dalí opened on 28 September with a flourish and a gala for the people of Figueres. Journalists, photographers, town dignitaries, government representatives and a thousand invited guests were there. Amanda Lear, whose collages were on show, stood at Dalí's side, next to the 80-year-old Gala who had had numerous face-lifts and was wearing a black wig. She was accompanied by the actor Jeff Fenholt, the star of *Jesus Christ Superstar*, whom she had flown in from New York for the occasion. They had been seen together in public since 1973 and for seven years Fenholt had spent the summers with Gala at her Púbol mansion. Dalí was awarded the highest honours and the Gold Medal of the Town of Figueres.

In his speech he said: *Our Caudillo has told me that this museum will become the Mecca of devotees of contemporary art. I want it to become the spiritual centre of Europe.* He then dedicated the dome 'to the rulers of Spain. […] In his 70th year and in the best of health, he was consecrating his museum–memorial-shrine-grave, in the tradition of the early kings of Spain.' [188]

Generalissimo Franco died on 20 November 1975. In 1947 Spain had already been declared a monarchy by a law of succession and in 1969 Juan Carlos, grandson of Alfonso XIII, was named as successor to the throne. Under him, King Juan Carlos I, Spain gradually transformed itself into a parliamentary democracy.

Within a few years the Teatro-Museo became the most popular museum in Spain after the Prado and 2000 people go through its rooms every day. A new will made by Salvador and Gala bequeathed their legacy of pictures to the museum and today these works from all his creative periods are shown in a special room.

For Dalí the opening of the museum symbolised a kind of life after death. He may have been anticipating his own demise, but what should be the shape of the earthly, bodily life of an 'immortal'? What was still to come – repetition? Naturally he was still painting and experimenting with the potentials of holography to introduce a third dimension onto flat canvas. He continued studying the painters he admired – Velázquez, Raphael and Michelangelo – and made magnificent copies of their works, while flirting with the possibility of making them look weird and exaggerated, by partially dissolving their colours, reconstructing them and adding surreal elements. New things were happening in his life as well. In early 1975 a film he had directed, *Impressions from Inner Mongolia*, was shown at Avoriaz in the French Alps and in June of that year he and the pyrotechnic Ruggieri mounted a firework spectacle on the Rhône at Avignon, which Dalí boasted was what the firework of his spirit looked like. In May 1977 the 22nd Salon de Montrouge showed a retrospective of his works and in 1979 he made his admission speech at the Académie des Beaux-Arts, when Tony Aubin greeted him as a new member and hailed him as a genius. Spanish television made a three-part programme about him.

At the age of 75 the great moments in his life were mostly receiving honours and attending receptions at retrospective exhibitions of his collected works. Dalí was reaping his well-deserved rewards. In December 1979 the Centre Georges Pompidou in Paris decided to mount a large retrospective – a privilege which had long been denied him, because he had supported Franco when the dictator ordered another five suspected terrorists to be shot only a few weeks before he died. (Dalí had apparently told a journalist at the time that freedom was shit, that Lenin had been against it, too, and that he personally was in favour of the Holy Inquisition, whereupon he had received letters with death threats, the house in Port Lligat was daubed with insults and stones were thrown through the windows. The Dalís had fled with Sabater to America.) [189]

The Pompidou exhibition comprised 169 paintings and 219 drawings, graphics and artefacts and Sabater had sent for some works which were lying uncatalogued in American depositories. A particular attraction was the *Kermesse Héroique (Heroic Village Fair)*, which filled the entire lower floor. It consisted of a Citroën hanging from the ceiling with Catalan butifarra blood sausages, and a spoon 32 metres long underneath it, into which water flowed from the car's radiator. There was also a reproduction of metro station entrances in art nouveau style. As art has to do with 'taste', Dalí often spoke of *edible beauty* (particularly about art nouveau) and may even have been thinking of the Catholic belief in transubstantiation.

In four months almost a million people visited the exhibition and when it moved to the Tate Gallery in London in the summer of 1980 it attracted some 8000 visitors a day. Pilgrims filed in procession past pictures from all his creative periods. If anyone had doubted it before, Dalí had now definitely become a phenomenon and a mirror of the kaleidoscope which was the 20th century.

In the catalogue, bound in cloth from the 'torn dress' which Dalí had designed for Elsa Schiaparelli in the 1930s, Pontus Hulten, the organiser, wrote: 'The great and unique personality of Salvador Dalí bestrode the frontiers of the aesthetic and revolutionary movement of surrealism. Dalí left it behind. Today he personifies it definitively and, at the same time, most elegantly, because he has adjusted surrealist painting to the majestic passing of time. Dalí embodies the anti-hero of today par excellence. His eccentricity, his exhibitionism, his flashes of genius, his spontaneous utterances, the strength with which he affirms or denies, his compulsions and his fears – all these exist in a society in which the outsider is the only valid constant, the perfect incarnation of lunacy. [...] Salvador Dalí has gone the whole way. His unique achievements are both striking and fascinating; they turn admiration for his work into a kind of godless worship, which finally transcends the person of the creator.' [190]

The events of the next years tell a sad story. Dalí became a lonely, sick old man who could not escape from his forlornness into his work, because after a prostate operation and a viral infection protracted by misusing medicaments (Gala, increasingly confused, gave him tranquillisers and pep-pills at random) his right arm had begun to shake and he had difficulty in painting. From 1981 on he could not travel any more but it was some consolation to him when in January 1982 King Juan Carlos bestowed on him the highest national honour of the Grand Cross of the Order of Charles III and in March he also received the highest regional distinction – the Gold Medal of the Catalan Government.

In the 1970s Dalí had begun to take an interest in scientific means for preserving life, such as cryogenics or conserving in helium, and in 1973, with a pinch of typical self-mockery, he designed a graphic folder containing *Ten Recipes for Immortality*. He then busied himself with the catastrophe theory of the mathematician René Thom.

Gala's tax situation was catastrophic, too. According to Dalí's biographer Ian Gibson, she lived in permanent fear of being prosecuted for massive tax arrears. Sabater's machinations also turned out to have been disastrous, for he had persuaded Dalí to sign a large number of blank sheets of paper, which could then be used at will to send the number of limited edition graphics sky-high. Buyers and art historians were soon to be occupied in finding out which were originals and which forgeries. The only people without a problem were the dealers.[191]

Life with Gala in the last years consisted principally of quarrels and unbridled hatred. When she died on 10 June 1982 at the age of 89, and at her own wish was embalmed and buried quietly in the crypt of Château Púbol, dressed in her favourite Dior dress, the catastrophe was complete. Dalí reacted by refusing to eat. Descharnes believed that it was a stratagem to bring himself through dehydration to a state in which his spirit would go on living for ever, and he had in fact been looking into such a theory in better times. As a result, for the rest of his life he was unable to swallow and had to be fed through a tube in his nose. He also lost his voice and could only communicate in whispers.

One more honour came his way. In July 1982 the title of Marqués de Dalí de Púbol was conferred on him by the king, whom Dalí had immortalised in his painting *The Prince of Sleep* in 1973-74 and who in 1981 had come with the Queen to visit him in Port Lligat.

Dalí was now living in a wing of the museum. In spite of his deteriorating health he still managed the business with the help of Descharnes, who had replaced the financially rapacious Sabater and now acted as Dalí's secretary. He became the painter's spokesman and negotiated his contracts, for instance for the Spanish perfume 'Salvador Dalí', which came in little bottles with a nose and a mouth. Among those next closest to him were Antoni Pitxot, the secretary Maria Theresa and Arturo Caminada. Arturo had been in his service since 1948 and was now his valet, nurse, chauffeur, dresser and the custodian of his properties, which comprised a garage in Cadaqués, a sheepfold converted into a hotel, the 'Coral de Gala', the house in Port Lligat and the Púbol mansion.

Bedridden, Dalí kept his nurses on the run by continually ringing his bell, until in 1984 a short circuit 'set his bed and his nightshirt on fire'.[192] Injured and in shock, he was taken to hospital and when he was discharged the television news showed an emaciated old man in a wheelchair. Viewers were moved by his barely audible words *Viva Espania, viva el Rei, viva Catalunya!*

*I have lived with death ever since I knew that I breathed. It is killing me with a cold relish which is only challenged by my vivid and lively passion to outlive myself in every minute and every infinitesimal second in which I am conscious of existing. This ceaseless, stubborn, wild and terrible tension is the whole story of my quest.*

*The game which amuses me most is to imagine that I am dead and being eaten by worms. I shut my eyes and see in incredible detail and with absolute, obscene precision how I am being slowly eaten up and digested by an infernal swarm of large, greenish maggots which feast on my flesh. They nest in my eye-sockets once they have nibbled up my eyeballs and start voraciously on my brain. I feel them on my tongue as they fall on it, slavering with pleasure. A breath of air under my ribs lifts my ribcage, while their masticatory organs destroy the network of my lungs. My heart offers a slight, token resistance; it has always served me well. It is like a huge sponge teeming with pus and suddenly it collapses, drowning in a magma in which fat white worms are swarming. [...] This is useful practice which I have undertaken since earliest childhood.* [193]

Salvador Dalí died on 23 January 1989. The game was over but the worms were going to have a difficult job: seven litres of formaldehyde were injected into his arteries, his corpse was embalmed, dressed in a beige silk tunic embroidered with a crown and a 'D' and laid in its coffin in the Torre Galatea of the museum. With mixed feelings, 15,000 citizens of his hometown of Figueres paid their last tribute to its world-famous son.

At his wish Dalí was buried in the crypt under the glass cupola of the Teatro-Museo and not next to Gala in the vault at Púbol. 'With his passion for god-kings and for the world of the Pharaohs, it was natural that, like them, he should have wanted to be buried with his playthings and to travel with them through eternity', wrote *La Vanguardia*.[194]

Dalí the man lives on in his works. Never before has his hometown attracted so many visitors. They are curious about the way this man expressed himself – this man who had dared to turn everything in the world on its head – often including himself.

# Notes

## Abbreviations

Dalí Retro = Salvador Dalí. Retrospektive 1920-1980. Gemälde, Zeichnungen, Grafiken, Objekte, Filme, Schriften. Munich 1993

Desch: Dalí = Robert Descharnes and Gilles Néret: Salvador Dalí, 1904-1989. L'oeuvre peint. Cologne, Benedikt Taschen, 2 vols 1993

D.L.B. = Dalí, Lorca Buñuel. Aufbruch in Madrid. Stuttgart 1993

Gibson = Ian Gibson: The Shameful Life of Salvador Dalí. London, Faber & Faber, 1997

S L = The Secret life of Salvador Dalí. New York, Dial Press 1942

Hocke = Gustav René Hocke: Die Welt als Labyrinth. Manier und Manie in der europäischen Kunst. Hamburg 1957

Lautréamont = Comte de Lautréamont: Les Chants de Maldoror. Paris, Gallimard 1973

. S D: Writings = Salvador Dalí: Declaration of the independence of the imagination and of everyone's rights to their own madness. Gesammelte Schriften, ed. Axel Matthes and Tilbert Diego Stegmann). Munich 1974

S D: Comment = Comment on devient Dalí. (The unspeakable confessions of Salvador Dalí.) Presented by André Parinaud. Paris, Robert Laffont 1973

| | | | |
|---|---|---|---|
| 1 | SL, p 49 | 14 | Gibson, p 25 |
| 2 | SL, p 50 | 15 | SL, p 92 ff |
| 3 | SL, p 494 | 16 | SL, p 96 |
| 4 | SL, p 11 | 17 | Set designs at Max Reinhardt's |
| 5 | SL, p 42 | | Deutsches Theater, Berlin |
| 6 | ibid. | 18 | SL, p 95 |
| 7 | SL, p 92 | 19 | SL, p 97ff |
| 8 | SL, p 51 | 20 | SL p 107 |
| 9 | ibid. A photo shows Salvador Dalí with about 80 pupils and their teacher, Trayter, dated '15 September 1908' | 21 | SL, p 108 |
| | | 22 | SL, p 110 |
| | | 23 | SL p 111ff |
| 10 | SL, p 53 | 24 | Nuñez had studied at the Royal Academy of Arts and won the Prix de Rome. He was especially known in his day for his perfect etchings |
| 11 | SL, p 55 | | |
| 12 | SL p 88 | | |
| 13 | SL p 90 | | |

25  SL, p 172
26  SL, p 156ff
27  SL, p 163
28  SL, p 164
29  SL, p 166
30  ibid
31  Gibson, p 66
32  SL, p 194
33  SL, p 187
34  ibid
35  SL, p 195
36  SL, p 196
37  Luis Buñuel: 'My Last Sigh. Memoirs'. Paris, Robert Laffont, 1982, p 43
38  Gibson, p 86
39  SD: Comment, p 57
40  ibid
41  SD: Comment, p 58
42  Ramón Gomez de la Serna: Greguerias, Berlin 1989, p 14ff
43  C G Jung, Karl Kerenyi, Paul Radin: Der göttliche Schelm. Ein indianischer Mythen- Zyklus.Zurich 1954, p 185
44  Dalí de Draeger: betw illus 162 and 163
45  Gibson, p 114
46  SD: 'Ich und die Malerei'.Confessions and conversations with Manuel del Arco. Zurich 1959, p 41
47  Desch: Dalí, p 84
48  D.L.B., p 64ff
49  D.L.B., p 65
50  ibid
51  Gibson, p 117. Ramón Gomez de la Serna had already published extracts from the 'Songs' in Spanish in 1909
52  Lautréamont, p 234
53  ibid
54  D.L.B., p 63
55  Gibson, p 135
56  D.L.B., p 162
57  D.L.B., p 42ff
58  D.L.B., p 136
59  Dalí de Draeger, after illus. 137
60  D.L.B., p 130
61  Gibson, p 138
62  Gibson, p 125
63  Gibson, p 37
64  SL, p 250
65  S.D.: Comment, p143ff
66  S.D. Writings, p 218ff. De la beauté terrifiante et comestible de l'architecture 'modern style.' Dalí had seen art nouveau work by the Catalonian architect Antoni Gaudí in Barcelona and they enraptured and inspired him
67  S.D.: Writings, p 16ff
68  S.D.: Writings, p 27
69  Dalí de Draeger, illus 14
70  Luis Buñuel: 'My last sigh'. Memoirs. Paris, Robert Laffont 1982.
71  S.D.: Writings, p 74
72  André Breton: 'Die magnetischen Felder; (1919). Heidelberg 1990
73  Philippe Soupault:'Ursprünge und Beginn des Surrealismus In: Surrealismus in Paris, ed. Karlheinz Barck.1919-39. Leipzig 1990, p 7
74  Gibson, p 188
75  From an interview given by Jose de la Colina and Tomas Perez Furret, published Oct-Nov 1980 in 'Contracampo', Madrid, no 16, p 33ff. (Quoted in Gibson p 193)
76  SL, p 268
77  SL, p 302
78  ibid
79  Catalogue of the Salvador Dalí Retrospective 1920-80, Centre Pompidou, Paris. Munich 1993, p124f
80  Paul Éluard: Lettres à Gala. Paris, Gallimard 1984
81  Apart from the Vicomte and Vicomtesse de Nouailles, the 'zodiac' consisted of Caresse Crosby, the architect Emilio Terry, the French-American writer Julien Green and his sister Anne, the Marquesa Margaret Cuevas de Vera, the illustrator André Durst, the Comtesse Anna Laetitia de Pecci- Blunt, René Laporte (Breton's publisher), Prince Faucigny-Lucinge, Félix Rolo and the diplomat Robert de Saint-Jean.
82  SL, p 328ff
83  Sl, p 324ff
84  S D: Writings, pp 288-291
85  S D: Writings, p 131
86  De la psychose paranoïque dans ses rapports avec la personnalité. Paris 1975. Cf Das Problem des Stils und

die psychiatrische Auffassung paranoischer Erlebnisformen. In S D: Writings, pp 352-256

87   S D: Writings, p 355
88   S D: Writings, p 196ff
89   S D: Writings, p 199
90   S D: Writings, p 202
91   Mark Polizotti: Revolution des Geistes. Das Leben André Bretons. Munich / Vienna 1996, p 569
92   ibid
93   Polizotti, op cit, p 572ff
94   Dawn Ades believed that *The last supper* by Heinrich Füssli (1781) encouraged Dalí to paint this picture. See Dawn Ades: 'Dalí's optical illusions', in 'Der endlose Rätsel. Dalí und der Magier der Mehrdeutigkeit', ed Jean-Hubert Martin and Stephan Andreae. Ostfildern-Ruit 2003, p 127
95   S D: Writings, p 132
96   Odilon Redon: 'A soi-même'. Quoted in Dalí Retro, p 245
97   S D: Writings, p 108
98   Exhibition catalogue: 'Der endlose Rätsel. Dalí und der Magier der Mehrdeutigkeit'. Kunst-Palast, Düsseldorf, 2003
99   Hocke, p 5
100  Hocke, p 53
101   S L, p 400
102  Desch: Dalí, p 213
103  Desch: Dalí, p 214ff
104   Desch: Dalí, p 218ff
105  Desch: Dalí, p 226
106  S D: Comment, p 202
107  Gibson, p 336
108  Gibson, p 341
109  Letter of 20 July 1938, Sigmund Freud to Stefan Zweig, quoted in Desch: Dalí, p 311ff. See also 'The Diary of Sigmund Freud', London 1992. pp 244 & 305
110  Not all works are included in Descharnes' and Néret's catalogue
111  Sunday News, 11 April, 1976. Interview with Judson Hand
112  Robert S Lubar: Dalí. The Salvador Dalí Museum Collection, Boston / New York / London 2000, p XI
113  The Weekly Newsmagazine,

Vol XXVIII, no 24
114  ibid, p XII
115   S L, p 444ff
116  Desch: Dalí, p 316. Descharnes stressed the part played by the telephone which was used prior to the Munich Treaty between Hitler and Chamberlain
117  The Diary of Anaïs Nin (1939-1944). New York 1969, p 39ff
118  op cit, p 40
119  Gibson, p 409
120  S L, p 446
121  Gibson, p 412
122  Desch: Dalí, p 348ff
123  The collection comprised 95 original oils, over 100 water colours and drawings and nearly 1300 graphics, apart from sculptures, artefacts, photographs, documents and a comprehensive library
124  Interview of the author with Mrs Eleanor Morse on 27 February 2003 in St Petersburg, Florida
125  Desch: Dalí, p 349ff
126  Salvador Dalí: 'Hidden Faces'. London, Nicholson and Watson 1947, p 212
127  op cit, p 10
128  op cit p 272ff
129  op cit, p 274
130   François Truffaut: 'Mr Hitchcock, how did you do it?' Munich 1973, p 154
131  Truffaut, op cit, p 155ff
132  Gibson, p 435
133  ibid
134  Salvador Dalí: '50 Secrets of Magic craftsmanship, New York, Dial Press 1948
135  op cit, p 9
136  op cit. p 53
137  S D: Comment, p 145
138  ibid
139  Desch: Dalí, p 477
140  Dalí Retro, p 372
141  ibid
142  op cit. p 373ff
143  op cit, p 363
144  A 14th century allegorical poem in 100 cantos and 14230 verses on this life and the after-life

145 Ralf Michler and Lutz W Löpsinger (eds): Dalí. Das druckgraphische Werk I: Radierungen and Mixed-Media-Graphiken 1924-80. Munich 1995, p 15

146 S D: Comment, p 282

147 ibid

148 op cit p 278

149 op cit, p 279

150 op cit, p 280

151 ibid

152 or *Young virgin, seduced by her own chastity*

153 or *The soft watches* or *The vanishing time,* 1931; 24 x 33 cm

154 Henri Bergson: 'Denken und schöpferisches Werden'. Meisenheim am Glan, 1948

155 Gendün Rinpoche: 'Herzensunterweisungen eines Mahamudra-Meister'. Berlin 2001, p 224ff

156 It comes as a surprise to see in a museum in their original format paintings, like *Narcissus* or the *Soft watches*, which have become famous through their reproductions

157 Desch: Dalí, p 768

158 This method of contributing to the creation of a picture through 'force of arms' has been taken up, for instance by the French painter and plasticist Niki de Saint Phalle

159 S D: Comment, p 282

160 Meryl Secrest: 'Salvador Dalí'. Bern / Munich / Vienna 1987, p 251

161 Tim McGirk: 'Gala. Dalí's skandalöse Muse'.Munich 1989, `p 199ff. Mara Albaretto, a friend of the Dalís, whom Gala frequently visited with Rotlein, maintained that they definitely had a sexual relationship

162 Op cit, p 196. Dalí loved to do the rounds at his parties. In every bedroom there were different couples – men with women, men with men, women with women. [...] Several important people were there – even French ministers

163 Gibson, p 502

164 Desch: Dalí, p 539

165 Susan Sontag: 'Art and anti-art'. Reinbek 1968

166 Gibson, p 499. Together with the older painters Bonaterra and Montoriol in 1918 and alone in 1919.

167 Wilhelm Salber: 'Bilder sind in Bewegung. Untersuchungen zu Marc, Dalí and Goya'. In: Commemorative publication for Heinrich Lützeler. Bonn 1987, pp 389-408

168 Gibson, p 507

169 Dalí de Draeger, index of pictures, no 118

170 Gibson, p 521ff

171 Desch: Dalí, p 567

172 Dalí Retro, p 444

173 Dalí Retro, before illus no 175

174 Amanda Lear: L'amant Dalí. Ma vie avec Salvador Dalí. Paris, Michel Lafon, 1994

175 Gibson, p 542

176 Luis Romero 'Todo Dalí en un rostro', Barcelona 1975. The Spanish writer describes the story behind the creation of the painting which Dalí liked to be called *All Dalí in one face.*

177 Desch: Dalí, p 580

178 The first decorative painting which entirely represented his new kitsch art was painted in the Alleuis palace in Barcelona and called *The royal lesson* (3m diameter)

179 Ramón Gómez de la Serna: 'A hologram is an image of an object, created by diffraction, which is lit with a beam of laser light to produce the complete illusion of a spatial impression'. Dalí. Eltville am Rhein 1981, p 65

180 R Buckminster Fuller: Bedienungsanleitung für das Raumschiff Erde and andere Schriften. Dresden 1998, ed Joachim Krause. Dresden 1998, p 274. Fuller's 'Expo-dome', a geodesic cupola 76m in diameter with a double-skinned network of thin metal supports and covered with light-reactive acrylic glass was the attraction of the 1967 Montreal Expo

181 First large-scale Dalí Retrospective at the Boymans-van Beuningen Museum, Rotterdam in 1970; Retrospective at the State Art Gallery Baden-Baden 1971; Dedication of the Dalí Museum in Cleveland, Ohio, March 1971

182 Gibson, p 544

183 The architects Ros de Ramis and Bonaterra Matra, who conceived the idea for the Picasso Museum in Barcelona, freed the arena of the theatre from all its previous clutter.

184 Desch: Dalí, p 611

185 Gibson, p 546

186 Gottfried Benn: 'Doppelleben'. Wiesbaden 1958, p 49

187 Chief of the Pawnee Indians; a colourful distortion of Charles Schreyvogel's 1899 sculpture

188 Eleonora Bairati: ' The Dalí Teatro-Museo in Figueres'. In: Ramón Gómez de la Serna: 'Dalí'. Eltville am Rhein, 1981, p 191

189 Gibson, p 561

190  Dalí Retro, p 5

191 Since 1994 there has been a 'complete, official and critical catalogue of Salvador Dali's graphic prints', which provides a guide. Ed: Ralf Michler and Lutz w Löpsinger: 'Salvador Dalí. Das druckgraphische Werk I: Oeuvrekatalog der Radierungen und Mixed-Media-Graphiken 1924-80. Munich – New York 1994, 954 plates. Das druckgraphische Werk II: Lithographien und Holzschnitte 1956-80. Munich / New York 1995, 1607 plates

192 Desch: Dalí, p 720

193 S D: comment, p 9

194 Gibson, p 620

## Translator's note

The original German-language edition was written in the present tense and in short sentences. To conform to the house style of the 'Life & Times' series of monographs, I have written in the past tense and in general in a more flowing style. I am deeply grateful to Dr Salber for her help with the in-depth psychiatric elements in her text, which I have taken the liberty to simplify for our English readership. AW

# Chronology

| Year | History | Culture |
|------|---------|---------|
| 1904 | France and Britain sign Entente Cordiale. Russo-Japanese War. Photoelectric cell invented. | Puccini *Madama Butterfly*. J M Barrie *Peter Pan*. Chekhov *The Cherry Orchard*. |
| 1908 | Bulgaria becomes independent. Austro-Hungary annexes Bosnia -Herzegovina. | Gustav Mahler *Das Lied von der Erde*. E M Forster *A Room with a View*. Cubism begins with Picasso and Braque. |
| 1912 | Balkan Wars. Titanic sinks. Republic of China founded. Stainless steel invented. | Arnold Schoenberg *Pierrot Lunaire*. Carl Jung *The Psychology of the Unconscious*. Bertrand Russell *The Problems of Philosophy*. |
| 1913 | Geiger counter invented. | Guillaume Apollinaire *Les peintres cubistes*. Marcel Proust *A la recherché du temps perdu*. D H Lawrence *Sons and Lovers*. |
| 1914 | Outbreak of First World War. | Pablo Picasso *Harlequin*. |
| 1916 | Easter Rising in Ireland. July-Nov: Battle of the Somme | Guillaume Apollinaire *Le Poète assassiné*. Dada movement launched in Zurich with Cabaret Voltaire. |
| 1917 | Russian Revolution; US enters war. Balfour Declaration | First recording of New Orleans jazz. Franz Kafka *Metamorphosis*. Giorgio de Chirico *Le Grand Métaphysique*. |
| 1918 | Execution of Russian Czar and family. End of First World War. Women's suffrage (over 18) in UK. 'Spanish flu' kills 20m people | Amédé Ozenfant and Le Corbusier *Après le Cubisme*. Oswald Spengler *The Decline of the West*. Paul Klee *Gartenplan*. |

| Year | Age | Life |
|------|-----|------|

1919   15   Sketches for a novel about an artist ('Summer Afternoons').

1920   16   Death of his mother; Dalí founds the socialist action group 'Renovacio Social' with his friends Martí Vilanova, Rafael Ramis and Jaume Miravitlles.

1921   17   January: Exhibition of eight pictures (all were sold) in a group exhibition at Josep Dalmau's Gallery in Barcelona; the Rector of Barcelona University awards him the painting prize. June: Gains his baccalauréat; participates in an exhibition of Empordá regional painters at the Casino Menestral in Figueres. October: Beginning of his studies at the San Fernando Academy of Fine Art in Madrid; lives at the 'Residencia de Estudiantes'; friendship with Luis Buñuel and Federico García Lorca.

1922   18   Riot at the Academy; Dalí suspended from his studies for a year; imprisoned for political reasons in Figueres and Girona from 21 May to 11 June.

1923   19   October: resumes studies in Madrid.

1924   20   Lorca visits Dalí in Cadaqués and Figueres; first one-man show (17 paintings and 5 drawings) in the Dalmau Gallery, 4-17 November; travels to Paris with his sister and aunt, where he visits Pablo Picasso in his studio.

1925   21   Expelled from the San Fernando Academy for improper behaviour, by royal decree of 20 October.

1927   23   Second one-man show, 31 December 1926-14 January 1927 at Dalmau Gallery; designs sets for Lorca's 'Mariana Pineda'; 1 February starts one year's military service in Figueres, but without the duties of an ordinary soldier; paints *Blood is Sweeter than Honey* (his first surrealist work); Joan Miró visits him in his studio.

1928   24   Second visit to Paris, meeting with André Breton and the surrealist group; three paintings shown in the International Exhibition at the Carnegie Institute, Pittsburgh, USA.

| Year | History | Culture |
|------|---------|---------|
| 1919 | Treaty of Versailles. Prohibition in US. Irish Civil War. | Bauhaus founded in Weimar. Franz Kafka *In the Penal Colony*. |
| 1920 | First meeting of League of Nations. | Edith Wharton *The Age of Innocence*. |
| 1921 | Irish Free State formed Mao Ze Dong helps found the Chinese Communist Party | Sergey Prokofiev *The Love of Three Oranges*. Luigi Pirandello *Six Characters in search of an Author*. |
| 1922 | Foundation of Soviet Union. Fascists march on Rome. | T S Eliot *The Waste Land*. James Joyce *Ulysses*. |
| 1923 | Military dictatorship of Primo de Rivera in Spain. | Le Corbusier *Vers une architecture*. |
| 1924 | Lenin dies. | E M Forster *A Passage to India*. André Breton's first *Surrealist Manifesto*. |
| 1925 | Campaign to unify China under Chiang Kai-shek. Discovery of the ionosphere. Television invented. | Erik Satie dies. Adolf Hitler *Mein Kampf*. Franz Kafka *The Trial*. Sergey Eisenstein *Battleship Potemkin*. |
| 1927 | Stalin comes to power. Charles Lindbergh flies across Atlantic. BBC public radio launched. | Virgina Woolf *To the Lighthouse*. Martin Heidegger *Being and Time*. |
| 1928 | Alexander Fleming discovers penicillin. | Kurt Weill *The Threepenny Opera*. Aldous Huxley *Point Counter Point*. D H Lawrence *Lady Chatterley's Lover*. Maurice Ravel *Boléro*. |

| Year | Age | Life |
|------|-----|------|

1929    25    Gala and Paul Éluard, Magritte and his wife and Buñuel visit Dalí in
              Cadaqués; writes screenplay for 'Un Chien Andalou' with Buñuel; film
              shown 11 October - 23 December at Studio 28, Paris; Works with Buñuel
              on screenplay for 'L'Age d'Or'; paints *The Great Masturbator;* falls out with
              his father; studio in Paris; living with Gala; 20 November - 5 December
              first Paris exhibition of 11 paintings in Goemans Gallery with catalogue
              foreword by Breton; intensive work with the surrealist group.

1930    26    Cover design for Breton's 'Second Surrealist Manifesto'; life with Gala in a
              fisherman's hut on the shore at Port Lligat; poems and theoretical essays
              about surrealist painting in the surrealists' journals; resignation of the
              dictator Primo de Rivera.

1931    27    Exhibition of *The Persistence of Memory* in Julien Levy's Gallery, New York.

1933    29    Group of collectors (the 'zodiac') ensures a regular income for Dalí;
              surrealist exhibition in the Colle Gallery, Paris (the 'surrealistic object'),
              followed by a Dalí one-man show; first one-man show at the Levy Gallery;
              exhibition at the Catalonia Gallery, Barcelona; Explanation of the
              'paranoiac-critical method' in 'The Conquest of the Irrational'.

1934    30    Dalí and Gala marry; tensions with Breton over the painting *The Enigma of
              William Tell;* travels to USA; exhibition at Levy Gallery; illustrations for
              'The Songs of Maldoror'; one-man show at Zwemmer Gallery, London
              Surrealist artefact exhibition (*The Aphrodisiacal Jacket*) in Charles Ratton
              Gallery, Paris; essays: 'The spectral surrealism of the Pre-Raphaelite eternal
              female and 'First morphological law of hairs on soft substances' (in
              'Minotaure'); Dalí on title page of 'Time'; exhibition at Levy's Gallery,
              many pictures sold on opening day (15 December); exhibition 'Fantastic
              Art, Dada and Surrealism', Museum of Modern Art, New York, organised
              by the Director, Alfred Barr.

1935    31    Meeting with Harpo Marx in Hollywood, *Portrait of Harpo Marx;*
              participates with eight paintings in the exhibition 'Origins and development
              of independent international art' in Jeu de Palme Museum, Paris; flight
              from Spanish Civil War; travels to Italy with Edward James (his patron until
              1939); paranoiac poem: 'The Metamorphosis of Narcissus'.

| Year | History | Culture |
|------|---------|---------|
| 1929 | Wall Street crash heralds Great Depression. | Robert Graves *Goodbye to all that.*<br> Ernest Hemingway *A Farewell to Arms.*<br>Erich Maria Remarque *All Quiet on the Western Front.*<br>Jean Cocteau *Les Enfants Terribles.* |
| 1930 | London Conference on India.<br>Mahatma Gandhi leads Salt March.<br>Turbo-jet engine patented.<br>Pluto discovered. | W H Auden *Poems.*<br>Evelyn Waugh *Vile Bodies.*<br>William Faulkner *As I lay dying.* |
| 1931 | King Alfonso XIII of Spain goes into exile; Spanish Republic formed. | |
| 1932 | | Aldous Huxley, *Brave New World* |
| 1933 | Nazis seize power in Germany – Hitler is Chancellor.<br>Roosevelt launches New Deal. | André Malraux *La condition humain.*<br>Gertrude Stein *The Autobiography of Alice B Toklas.* |
| 1934 | Night of Long Knives in Germany.<br>Long March in China.<br>First controlled nuclear reaction. | Dmitri Shostakovich *Lady Macbeth of Mtsensk.*<br>Agatha Christie *Murder on the Orient Express.*<br>Henry Miller *Tropic of Cancer.* |
| 1935 | Racial Laws enacted in Germany.<br>Italy invades Abyssinia. | George Gershwin *Porgy and Bess.*<br>Christopher Isherwood *Mr Norris changes Trains.*<br>Marx Brothers *A Night at the Opera.* |

| Year | Age | Life |
|------|-----|------|

1936   32   Surrealist exhibition (André Breton and Paul Éluard) in Paris with Dalí's 'Taxi Pluvieux' ('Rainy taxi'); meets Sigmund Freud in London.

1937   33   'Night and Day' – window display for Bonwit Teller, New York; exhibition at Levy Gallery (painting *Debris of a Motorcar Giving Birth to a Blind Horse Chewing up a Telephone* attracts attention); walk-in sculpture-event 'Dream of Venus' for New York World Exhibition; 'Declaration of the Independence of the Imagination and the Rights of Man to his own Madness'; production and designs for 'Bacchanal' at Metropolitan Opera, New York.

1938   34   When the Germans invade France, Dalí and Gala leave Europe for the USA.

1939   35   Autobiography 'The secret Life of Salvador Dalí'; collaboration with photographer Philippe Halsman; ballet 'Labyrinth' at Metropolitan Opera; retrospective of Dalí and Miró at Museum of Modern Art, New York; jewellery designs New York exhibition shown in eight major American cities; photo-reportage in 'Click' magazine.

1940   36   Exhibition of portraits of American personalities at Knoedler Gallery, New York.

1941   37   Novel 'Hidden Faces'; designs for ties; advertisements for Bryan Hosiery; sets, costumes and curtain with cyclists for the ballet 'Sentimental Colloquy' at International Theater, New York, music by Paul Bowles; sets and costumes for 'Tristan Fou', idea by Dalí from Wagner's *Tristan und Isolde: First Paranoiac Ballet based on the Myth of Love leading to Death.*

1942   38   Dream sequence for Hitchcock's 'Spellbound'; first number of 'Dalí News. Monarch of the Dailies' on the occasion of his exhibition at Bignou Gallery, New York.

| Year | History | Culture |
|------|---------|---------|
| 1936 | Spanish Civil War breaks out. Germany occupies Rhineland. Edward VIII abdicates. | Sergey Prokofiev *Peter and the Wolf.* A J Ayer *Language, Truth and Logic.* |
| 1937 | Japan invades China. Arab-Jewish conflict in Palestine. | Pablo Picasso *Guernica.* Jean-Paul Sartre *La Nausée.* John Steinbeck *Of Mice and Men.* |
| 1938 | Soviet political trials. Kristallnacht. Austro-German Anschluss. Munich crisis. Germany invades Czechoslovakia. IRA bombings in England. Nuclear fission discovered. | Graham Greene *Brighton Rock.* Elizabeth Bowen *The Death of the Heart.* Sergey Eisenstein *Alexander Nevsky.* |
| 1939 | Spanish Civil War ends; Francisco Franco becomes dictator of Spain. Russo-German Non-Aggression Pact. Germany invades Poland. World War II breaks out. | John Steinbeck *The Grapes of Wrath.* David O Selznick *Gone with the Wind.* |
| 1940 | Germany overruns Western Europe. Retreat from Dunkirk. Churchill becomes UK prime minister. Battle of Britain. Trotsky assassinated. | Ernest Hemingway *For whom the Bell tolls.* Charlie Chaplin *The Great Dictator.* Walt Disney *Fantasia.* |
| 1941 | Germany invades Soviet Union. Italians driven out of Africa. US Lend-Lease Bill passed. Atlantic Charter signed Japan attacks Pearl Harbour, US enters the war. | Bertolt Brecht *Mother Courage and her Children.* Orson Welles *Citizen Kane.* |
| 1942 | Wannsee Conference plots extermination of Jews from Europe; German Sixth Army encircled in Stalingrad. | Albert Camus *L'Etranger.* Jean Anouilh *Antigone.* |

| Year | Age | Life |
|------|-----|------|
| 1943 | 39 | Exhibition at Knoedler Gallery of eleven pictures on the theme of the Temptation of St Anthony for a competition organised by Loew-Levin film company, which is won by Max Ernst; illustration for Shakespeare's 'Macbeth'; designs title page for Christmas number of 'Vogue'. |
| 1944 | 40 | Illustration for Montaigne's 'Essays'; one-man show at Cleveland Museum of Art; collaboration with Walt Disney. |
| 1945 | 41 | '50 Secrets of Magical Craftsmanship'; 21 July: return to Europe and to Port Lligat; Spanish journal 'Destino' dedicates to him an article 'Bienvenido Salvador Dalí'; sets and costumes for Shakespeare's 'As you like it' in Rome, directed by Luchino Visconti; exhibition in Galleria del Obelisco, Rome; Dalí converts to Catholicism. |
| 1946 | 42 | Sets for London production of Richard Strauss's 'Salome', directed by Peter Brook; private audience with Pope Pius XII; *Madonna of Port Lligat*. |
| 1947 | 43 | Sets and costumes for 'Don Juan Tenorio' by Torilla in María Guerrero Theatre, Madrid; exhibition in Carstairs Gallery, New York. |
| 1948 | 44 | 'Mystical Manifesto' on display in Berggruen's bookshop, Paris. |
| 1949 | 45 | Death of his father; lecture tour of the USA with presentation of 'nuclear mysticism' and 'atomic art'. |
| 1954 | 50 | Retrospective in Rome with 41 works from all his creative periods and 102 water colours for Dante's 'Divine Comedy'; film with Robert Descharnes: 'The Prodigious History of the Lacemaker and the Rhinoceros'; 'Dalí's Moustache' (book by Dalí and Philippe Halsmann) appears in New York; exhibition at Carstairs Gallery of works from previous six months. |

| Year | History | Culture |
|------|---------|---------|
| 1943 | Allied invasion of Italy. Mussolini deposed. Teheran Conference. Hallucinogenic properties of LSD discovered. | Rodgers and Hammerstein *Oklahoma*. Jean-Paul Sartre *Being and Nothingness*. T S Eliot *Four Quartets*. |
| 1944 | Allies land in France and liberate Paris. Civil War in Greece. | Jorge Luis Borges *Fictions*. Sergey Eisenstein *Ivan the Terrible*. |
| 1945 | Yalta Agreement. Germany surrenders. United Nations formed. Potsdam Conference. Atomic bombs dropped on Hiroshima and Nagasaki. Japan surrenders. UNESCO formed. | Benjamin Britten *Peter Grimes*. George Orwell *Animal Farm*. |
| 1946 | Italian Republic formed. Nuremberg Trials open. | Jean-Paul Sartre *Existentialism and Humanism*. Bertrand Russell *History of Western Philosophy*. Jean Cocteau *La Belle et la Bête*. |
| 1947 | India becomes independent. Sound barrier broken. | Tennessee Williams *A Streetcar named Desire*. Albert Camus *The Plague*. Jean Genet *The Maids*. |
| 1948 | Marshall Plan launched. Apartheid begins in South Africa. | Bertold Brecht *The Caucasian Chalk Circle*. Norman Mailer **The Naked and the Dead.** Alan Paton *Cry, the beloved Country*. Vittorio de Sica *Bicycle Thieves*. |
| 1949 | Nato founded. Republic of Ireland formed. People's Republic of China established. | George Orwell *1984*. Simone de Beauvoir *The Second Sex*. Arthur Miller *Death of a Salesman*. |
| 1953 | Stalin dies. Egyptian Republic formed. Mau Mau rebellion in Kenya. Korean War ends. Double helix DNA structure discovered. Colour television service begins in US. | Dylan Thomas *Under Milk Wood*. Federico Fellini *I Vitelloni*. Arthur Miller *The Crucible*. |

| Year | Age | Life |
|------|-----|------|
| 1955 | 51 | Lecture at the Sorbonne, Paris: 'Phenomenal aspects of the Paranoiac-critical Method'. |
| 1956 | 52 | Private audience with General Franco in Bardo Palace, Madrid; exhibition of *The Last Supper* and other paintings in the Chester Dale Collection, National Gallery, Washington; retrospective in Knokke-le-Zoute. |
| 1957 | 53 | Exhibition of illustrations for 'Don Quixote' at Jacquemart-André Museum, Paris; Walt Disney visits Dalí at Port Lligat. |
| 1958 | 54 | Church marriage ceremony with Gala in the Sanctuary of Our Lady of the Angels at Sant Martí Vell. |
| 1959 | 55 | Audience with Pope John XXIII; invents 'bulletism' (his form of 'tachism', involving shooting at copper plates) to produce *The Revelation of St John the Divine*. |
| 1960 | 56 | Surrealist tract 'We don't EAR it that way' against Dalí's participation in the international exhibition of surrealist art in the D'Arcy Gallery, New York with *The Sistine Madonna*. |
| 1961 | 57 | Joseph Forêt's edition of the 'Divine Comedy' with Dalí's lithographs exhibited at the Musée d'Art Moderne, Paris; fiesta in Dalí's honour; ballet 'Gala' with idea, sets and costumes by Dalí and choreography by Maurice Béjart performed in Venice. |
| 1962 | 58 | Inspired by 19th century historical painters Fortuny and Meissonier to invent 'pompierism'. |
| 1963 | 59 | 'The Tragic Myth of Millet's *Angelus*': Dalí's paranoiac-critical analysis of the painting (1933) republished in Paris. |
| 1964 | 60 | Dalí awarded the highest Spanish honour of the Grand Cross of Queen Isabella of Spain; retrospective at Seibu Museum, Tokyo. |

| Year | History | Culture |
|------|---------|---------|
| 1955 | Germany joins Nato.<br>Warsaw Pact formed. | Vladimir Nabokov *Lolita*. |
| 1956 | Khruschev denounces Stalin.<br>Suez crisis.<br>Castro and Guevara land in Cuba.<br>Revolts in Poland and Hungary.<br>Vietnam War. | Loewe and Lerner *My Fair Lady*.<br>Elvis Presley *Love me tender*.<br>John Osborne *Look back in Anger*. |
| 1957 | Treaty of Rome to found EEC.<br>Sputnik I launched. | Bernstein and Sondheim *West Side Story*.<br>Francis Poulenc *Les Dialogues des Carmelites*. |
| 1958 | De Gaulle becomes French President.<br>John XXIII elected Pope.<br>Great Leap Forward in China.<br>Silicon chip invented. | Boris Pasternak *Dr Zhivago*.<br>Harold Pinter *The Birthday Party*.<br>J K Galbraith *The Affluent Society*. |
| 1960 | Sharpeville Massacre in S Africa.<br>Vietnam War begins. | Federico Fellini *La Dolce Vita*.<br>Alfred Hitchcock *Psycho*. |
| 1961 | Berlin Wall erected.<br>Bay of Pigs invasion.<br>Gagarin first man in space.. | Rolling Stones formed.<br>Rudolf Nureyev defects.<br>François Truffaut *Jules et Jim*. |
| 1962 | Cuban missile crisis.<br>Second Vatican Council.<br>Satellite television launched. | Alexander Solzhenitsyn *One Day in the Life of Ivan Denisovich*.<br>Edward Albee *Who's afraid of Virginia Woolf*.<br>David Lean *Lawrence of Arabia*. |
| 1963 | Kennedy assassinated.<br>Civil Rights march in US.<br>Nuclear test-ban treaty. | The Beatles *She Loves you* and *I want to hold your hand*.<br>Luchino Visconti *The Leopard*. |
| 1964 | First Race Relations Act in UK,<br>Civil Rights Act in US.<br>Word processor invented. | Saul Bellow *Herzog*.<br>Philip Larkin *The Whitsun Weddings*.<br>Stanley Kubrick *Dr Strangelove*. |

| Year | Age | Life |
|------|-----|------|
| 1965 | 61 | Work on holographic pictures; exhibition at Knoedler Gallery with *The Station of Perpignan*; grand retrospective at Gallery of Modern Art, New York (170 paintings, 60 drawings, graphic prints, plastics and artefacts). |
| 1967 | 63 | 'Homage to Meissonier' at Hotel Meurice, Paris with presentation of *Tuna Fishing* . |
| 1968 | 64 | 'My Passions' by Dalí and Louis Pauwels and 'Dalí de Draeger' appear in Paris; during the May riots in Paris Dalí takes the students' side with the pamphlet 'My Cultural Revolution'; Musée Grevin accepts a Dalí sculpture of Barbieri into its collection of portraits of famous personalities. |
| 1969 | 65 | Publication of the 'Erotic Metamorphoses'; television commercial for Chocolat Lanvin; at the annual conference of Parisian lawyers, Dalí enters into verbal battle over the question: 'Has an artist, who attributes the worth and originality of his work to the paranoiac state which he believes has befallen him, the right to accuse a journalist of libel for asserting in a newspaper article that the professional success of this artist proves that he is in exceptionally robust good mental health?' |
| 1970 | 66 | Press conference at Musée Gustave Moreau, Paris to announce the foundation of a Dalí museum in Figueres; poster designs for French Railways; retrospective in Boymans-van Beuningen Museum, Rotterdam. |
| 1971 | 67 | Retrospective in State Gallery, Baden-Baden; dedication of the Dalí Museum in Cleveland, Ohio (Morse Collection); design for the Christmas number of the French edition of 'Vogue' with double portrait of Marilyn Monroe and Mao Tse-tung. |
| 1972 | 68 | Hologram at Knoedler Gallery; illustrations for Boccaccio's 'Decameron'. |
| 1974 | 70 | Retrospective at Städelsche Kunstinstitut, Frankfurt; 'Comment on devient Dalí' ('The Unspeakable Confessions of Salvador Dalí') by Dalí and Parinaud; dedication of the Teatro-Museo Dalí in Figueres. |

| Year | History | Culture |
|------|---------|---------|
| 1965 | Indo-Pakistan War. | Harold Pinter *The Homecoming.* The Beach Boys *California Girls.* |
| 1967 | Six Day War. First heart transplant. | Tom Stoppard *Rosencrantz and Guildenstern are dead.* Gabriel Garcia Marquez *One Hundred Years of Solitude.* |
| 1968 | Martin Luther King and Robert Kennedy assassinated. Student riots in Paris. | Stanley Kubrick *2001.* |
| 1969 | First man on the moon. Anti-war rallies in US. US Dept of Defence creates internet. | Kenneth Clark *Civilisation.* Mario Puzo *The Godfather.* |
| 1970 | Charles de Gaulle dies. Antonio Salazar dies. Gamel Abd el Nasser dies. | Simon and Garfunkel *Bridge over troubled Water.* Germaine Greer *The Female Eunuch.* |
| 1971 | Willy Brandt awarded Noel Peace Prize. Indira Ganhi elected Prime Minister of India | Alexander Solzhenitsyn *August 1914.* Benjamin Britten *Owen Wingrave.* Stanley Kubrick *A Clockwork Orange.* |
| 1972 | US recognises Communist China. Bloody Sunday massacre in N Ireland. Pinochet takes power in Chile. World Trade Centre completed. Optical fibre invented. | Richard Adams *Watership Down.* Bertolucci *Last Tango in Paris.* |
| 1973 | Yom Kippur War. OPEC oil crisis. | Philip Larkin *High Windows.* E F Schumacher *Small is beautiful.* |
| 1974 | Watergate scandal in US. Solzhenitsyn expelled from USSR. | Dario Fo *Can't Pay? Won't Pay.* |

| Year | History | Culture |
|------|---------|---------|
| 1975 | Franco dies; Juan Carlos becomes King of Spain. End of Vietnam War. Apollo and Soyuz dock in space. | Boulez *Rituel in memoriam Bruno Maderna*. Steven Spielberg *Jaws* |
| 1976 | Chairman Mao dies. Soweto massacre. | Alex Haley *Roots*. |
| 1977 | Democratic elections in Spain. Steve Biko murdered in S Africa. | George Lucas *Star Wars*. Elvis Presley dies. |
| 1978 | John Paul II elected pope. Camp David Accord. Boat people leave Vietnam. First test-tube baby born. | Lloyd Webber and Rice *Evita*. Iris Murdoch *The Sea, the Sea*. |
| 1979 | Soviet Union invades Afghanistan. | Woody Allen *Manhattan*. Terry Jones *Monty Python's Life of Brian*. |
| 1982 | Spain joins Nato and socialists win election; miliarly court sentences leader of 1981 attempted coup to 30 years in jail; military deployed against ETA terrorists. Falklands Islands War. Compact discs introduced. | Beuys installations at the Documenta. Garcia Marquez awarded Nobel Prize for Literature. Richard Attenborough *Gandhi*. Steven Spielberg *ET*. Luciano Berio *La Vera Storia*. |

# Bibliography

LISTS OF WORKS AND BIBLIOGRAPHIES

Descharnes, Robert and Gilles Néret: *Salvador Dalí 1904-1989. L'oeuvre peint.* Cologne,
    Benedikt Taschen, (2 vols) 1993
Michler, Ralf and Lutz W Löpsinger (editors): *Dalí. Das druckgraphische Werk I:
    Oeuvrekatalog der Radierungen und Mixed-Media-Graphiken 1924-80.*
            Das druckgraphische Werk II: Lithographien und Holzschnitte 1956-80.
    Munich 1995
Field, Albert: *The Official Catalog of the graphic works of Salvador Dalí.* New York 1996

CATALOGUES (SELECTION)

Fanés, Fèlix: *Dalí. Architecture.* Madrid 1996
Gímenez-Frontín, J L: *Teatre-Museu Dalí.* Fundació Gala-Salvador Dalí. Madrid 2001
Hüngerle, Rudolf A (Ed): *Salvador Dalí. Gemälde Zeichnungen Objekte Skulpturen.*
    Exhibition at Heidelberg Castle, 2.10 – 4.11.1981. Plankstadt nr Heidelberg, 1981
Lubar, Robert S: *Dalí. The Salvador Dalí Museum Collection.* Boston – New York –
    London 2000
Martin, Jean-Hubert and Stephan Andreae: *The endless enigma. Dalí and the Wizard of
    Ambiguity.* Ostfildern-Ruit 2003
Maur, Karin von: *Salvador Dalí. 1904-89.* Staatsgalerie Stuttgart 13.5 – 13.7.1989 and
    Kunsthaus Zurich 18.8 – 22.10.1989. Stuttgart 1989
*Salvador Dalí Dream of Venus.* Teatro Museo Dalí, Figueres, Spain. 20.12.1999 –
    28.2.2000. Museum of Contemporary Art, North Miami (Florida). 14.3.2002 –
    30.6.2002
*Salvador Dalí Retrospektive 1920-80.* Gemälde, Zeichnungen, Grafike, Objekte,  Filme,
    Schrifte. Munich 1993
The Salvador Dalí Foundation: *Dalí: The Salvador Dalí Museum Collection.* Foreword by
    A Reynolds Morse. Boston – Toronto – London 1991

SALVADOR DALÍ'S WRITINGS (SELECTION)

Dalí, Salvador: *Painting and me. Confessions and Conversations with Manuel del Arco*. Zurich 1959
- with Louis Pauwels *The Passions according to Dalí*. Trans Eleanor Morse. The Salvador Dalí Museum, St Petersburg, Florida 1985
- *Declaration of the independence of the imagination and of the rights of everyone to their own madness*. New York 1939
- *Hidden Faces*. (novel) trans Haakon Chevalier. London, Nicholson and Watson 1947
- *50 Secrets of Magic Craftsmanship*. New York, Dial Press, 1948
- *The Secret Life of Salvador Dalí*. New York, 1942
- *The Diary of a Genius*. London, Hutchinson 1966
- *Dalí de Draeger*. Paris 1969
- with Philippe Halsman: *Dalí's Moustache*. Paris, Flammarion 1994
- *Comment on devient Dalí. The Unspeakable Confessions of Salvador Dalí*, to André Parinaud trans Harold J. Salemson. New York, William Morrow 1976
Torroella, Rafael Santos (ed): *'Los putrefactos' de Dalí y Lorca. Historia y antologia de un libro que no pudo ser*. Madrid 1998

SURREALISM

Barck, Karlheinz (ed): Philippe Soupault: *Origins and Beginnings of Surrealism*. In 'Surrealism in Paris 1919-1939'
Becker, Heribert (ed): *'Das heisse Raubtier'. Erotik und Surrealismus*. Munich – New York 1998
Breton, André: *'Communicating Pipes'*. Munich 1973
- *Le Manifeste du surrealisme*. Edited by Jürgen Manthey. Reinbek 1977
- (with André Parinaud and others) *Entretiens 1952*. Trans as *'Conversations. The Autobiography of Surrealism'* by Mark Polizotti New York, Paragon House 1993
Breton, André and Philippe Soupault: *'Die magnetischen Felder (1919)*. Heidelberg 1990
Glozer, László: *Picasso und der Surrealismus*. Cologne 1974
Kellerer, Christian: *Objet trouvé und Surrealismus. Zur Psychologie der modernen Kunst*. Reinbek 1968
Kunsthalle Vienna and Museo Nacional Centro de Arte Reina Sofia, Madrid. *The lugubrious Game. Surrealism in Spain 1924-1939*. Stuttgart 1995
Lebel, Sanouillet and Waldberg: *Surrealism, Dadaism and metaphysical Painting*. Cologne 1987
Nadeau, Maurice: *The History of Surrealism*. Introd. Roger Shattuck. New York, Collier Books 1967
Polizotti, Mark (ed): Julien Levy: *Surrealism*. New York 1995
Sawin, Martica: *Surrealism in Exile and the Beginnings of the New York School*. Cambridge, Mass – London 1995
Schwarz, Arturo (ed): *Die Surrealisten*. Frankfurt 1989
Spies, Werner (ed): *Surrealismus 1919-44*. Ostfildern-Ruit 2002
Waldberg, Patrick: *Surrealism*. London, Thames & Hudson 1965

BIOGRAPHIES

Cowles, Fleur: *Dalí. The case of Salvador Dalí.* Heinemann, London 1959
Dalí, Ana Maria: *Salvador Dalí visto por su hermana.* Barcelona 1949. Trans as '*Salvador Dalí seen by his sister*' by Griselda Boler. Typescript in the research Library, Dalí Museum, St Petersburg, Florida
Etherington-Smith, Meredith: *Dalí. A biography.* Sinclair-Stevenson, London 1992
Genzmer, Herbert: *Dalí und Gala. Der Maler und die Muse.* Berlin 1998
Lear, Amanda: *Le Dalí d'Amanda.* Paris, Favre 1984. Reprinted as '*L'amant Dalí. Ma vie avec Salvador Dalí*', Paris, Michel Lafon 1994
Gibson, Ian: *The Shameful Life of Salvador Dalí.* London, Faber and Faber 1997
McGirk, Tim: *Wicked lady: Salvador Dalí's muse.* London, Hutchinson 1989
Secrest, Meryl: *Salvador Dalí.* New York, E P Dutton 1986


STUDIES

Ades, Dawn and Bradley, Fiona: *Salvador Dalí. A mythology.* London 1998
Bokelberg, Werner: *Da Da Dalí.* Bremen 1966
Descharnes, Robert: *Salvador Dalí.* Trans Eleanor Morse. London, Thames & Hudson 1985
Fanés Fèlix: *Salvador Dalí. La construcción de la imagen 1925-1930.* Madrid 1999
Gómez de la Serna, Ramón: *Dalí. 'Epilogue*' by Balthasar Porcel. Madrid, Espasa-Calpe 1977
Larkin, David (ed): *Dalí.* Hamburg – New York 1974
Morse, A Reynolds: *Dalí. The masterworks.* Cleveland, Ohio 1971
Néret, Gilles: *Dalí.* Cologne 2002
Radford, Robert: *Dalí.* London – New York 2001
Schiebler, Ralf: Dalís Begierde. Munich – New York 1996


FURTHER READING

Aub, Max: *Conversaciones con Buñuel, seguidas de 45 entrevistas con familiares, amigos y colaboradores del cineasta aragonés.* Prologue by Federico Alvarez. Madrid, Aguilar, 1985
Banz, Helmut W and Alice Goetz: *Luis Buñuel. Documentation.* Bad Ems 1965
Barral i Altet, Xavier: *Die Geschichte der spanischen Kunst.* Cologne 1997
Benn, Gottfried: *Doppelleben.* Wiesbaden 1958
Bergson, Henri: *Denken und schöpferisches Werden.* Meisenheim am Glan 1948
Buñuel, Luis: *Mon Dernier Soupir (My Last Sigh).* Paris, Robert Laffont, 1982
Elliot, J H: *Die spanische Welt.* Geschichte, Kultur, Gesellschaft. Freiburg / Basle / Vienna 1991
Éluard, Paul: *Hauptstadt der Schmerzen.* Berlin, no year
- *Lettres à Gala (1924-48).* Ed Pierre Dreyfus, preface by Jean-Claude Carrière. Paris, Gallimard 1984
Finaldi, Gabriele (ed): *The Image of Christ.* London 2000

Fuchs, Ernst: *Phantastisches Leben. Memoirs.* Berlin 2001

García Lorca, Federico: *Verse Dramas.* Wiesbaden 1954

-   *Poems.* Frankfurt 1969

Gibson, Ian: *Federico García Lorca. A life.* London, Faber & Faber, 1989

Gómez de la Serna, Ramón: *Greguerias. Selección 1949-52.* Madrid, Espasa-Calpe, 1952

Haftmann, Werner: *Malerei im 20. Jahrhundert.* Munich 1965

Hocke, Gustav René: *Die Welt als Labyrinth. Manier und Manie in der europäischen Kunst.* Hamburg 1957

Jung, C G, Karl Kerenyi und Paul Radin: *Der göttliche Schelm.* Ein indianischer Mythen-Zyklus. Zurich 1954

Krausse, Joachim (ed): R Buckminster Fuller: *Bedienungsanleitung für das Raumschiff Erde und andere Schriften.* Dresden 1998

Lautréamont, Comte de (Isidore Ducasse): *Les chants de Maldoror.* Spanish translation: 'Los cantos de Maldoror par el Conde de Lautréamont by Ramón Gómez de la Serna. Madrid, Biblioteca Nueva. No date

Parrot, Louis: *Paul Éluard. Portrait et poésie.* Neuwied – Berlin 1963

Polizotti, Mark: *Revolution des Geistes. Das Leben André Bretons.* Munich / Vienna 1996

Prieto, Gregorio (ed): *Federico García Lorca. Zeichnungen.* Zurich 1961

Raeburn, Michael (ed): *Homage to Barcelona. The City and its Art 1888-1936.* London 1986

Redon, Odilon. *A soi-même.* Quoted in Salvador Dalí. Retrospektive 1920-80

Rinpoche, Gendün: *Herzensunterweisungen eines Mahamudra-Meisters.* Berlin 2001

Romero, Luis: *Todo Dalí en un rostro.* Barcelona 1975

Salber, Linde: *Frida Kahlo.* Reinbek 1997

Anaïs Nin. *Tausendundeine Frau.* Giessen 2002

Salber, Linde und Schulte, Arnim (ed): *Traum – Träume – Träumen.* Giessen 2001

Salber, Wilhelm: *Bilder sind in Bewegung.* Studies of Marc, Dalí and Goya in Commemorative Address for Heinrich Lützeler. Bonn 1987

-   *Psychästhetik.* Cologne 2002

Schenk, Amelie: *Schamanen. Auf dem Dach der Welt.* Trance- Heilung – Initiation. Graz 1994

Schiebler, Ralf (ed): *Dalí Lorca Buñuel. Aufbruch in Madrid.* Stuttgart 1993

Schmied, Wieland: *De Chirico und sein Schatten. Metaphysische und surrealistische Tendenzen in der Kunst des 20. Jahrhunderts.* Munich 1989

Schneede, Uwe M: *Die Geschichte der Kunst im 20. Jahrhundert. Von den Avantgarden bis zur Gegenwart.* Munich 2001

Sontag, Susan: *Art and Anti-art.* Reinbek 1968

Spies, Werner: *Max Ernst. Collages.* Paris – Cologne 1988

-   *Kontinent Picasso.* Munich 1988

Truffaut, François: *Mr Hitchcock, how did you do it?* Munich 1973

Walther, Ingo F (ed): *Kunst des 20. Jahrhunderts. Teil I: Karl Ruhrberg: Malerei.* Cologne

# Picture Sources

The author and publishers wish to express their thanks to the following sources of illustrative material and/or permission to reproduce it. They will make the proper acknowledgements in future editions in the event that any omissions have occurred.

AKG-Images: pp. 42, 133.
Bridgeman Art Collection: pp. 7, 39, 44, 47, 51, 59, 62, 73, 74, 94, 101, 112.
Lebrecht Picture Library/Rue des Archives: pp. i iii, 5, 12, 20, 27, 53, 68, 78, 83, 86, 88, 91, 97, 99, 100, 103, 104, 106, 107, 108, 114, 117, 122.

# Testimonials

JULIEN GREEN
*French-American writer and one of the 'zodiac'*

I lose myself in gazing on this marvellous world where one is drawn back into one's most distant childhood dreams. The impression which this extraordinary universe conjures up is strange, but 'possible'; it seems somehow to spread a quietness and develops within this quietness like a plant in a flood of light.
1932

MAURICE NADEAU
*Writer*

By joining the movement [surrealism] Dalí gave it the bloom of second youth by letting it start afresh on its old tracks of the all-powerful spirit which on the strength of its exaltation could nevertheless give arbitrary form to the unrelentingly opposed world of facts. The surrealists could acknowledge that they had solved this problem, once they felt the strength to intrude upon objects and to fashion them according to their own, unconscious desires.
1945

WERNER HAFTMANN
*Art historian*

Through Salvador Dalí veristic surrealism received its ultimate expression. Dalí opposed the passivity of inventing automatic images with a hysterical, raging and indefatigable power of association by transforming, displacing and dismantling. […] So in front of broad landscapes with their steep, disturbing perspectives rise desolate monuments made of putrid heaps of pieced together limbs, grotesque human beings hang broodingly like balloons in motionless air, solid objects dissolve gently and change their volume, watch faces hang like rubbery cloths over grotesque rubble. The frightening thing about this descriptive art is the lack of human participation, the ticking, registering of a gadget superimposed onto the phenomenon of the absurd, the lack of horror, the cold, cerebral curiosity which is manifested with the utmost objectivity out of the murkiest realm of the instinctive world of erupting images.
1954

MANUEL DEL ARCO
*Barcelona journalist and collabroator*

Dalí's sin – which is not a sin – is the obsession that he must always come first, which dogged him throughout his life. If he had confined himself just to painting in seclusion, only coming out of his hole to show his pictures, so that no one knew anything about his life and his eccentricities, everything he produced would certainly have appeared to his detractors to be works of genius.
1959

ANDRÉ PARINAUD
*Author and collaborator*

If Nietzsche had known Dalí he would have felt he had met his superman, his Zarathustra, through Dalí's will to power, his constant rising beyond himself, his over-acute understanding and the challenges which he continuously hurled at death, morals, the establishment and human beings. History as it comes to us through literature or legendary memories knows few examples of an existence which asserted itself so shamelessly in its total lack of moderation, or of an intelligence so sharp that it could intensify into a paroxysm of clairvoyant delirium. In more than one way the phenomenon which was Dalí is exemplary: the artist is prodigious, the psychologist an inexhaustible mine, the intellectual encyclopaedic, the man is fascinating and his success is glorious.
1973

WERNER SPIES
*Art historian*

If you mention Dalí's name, people smile with pleasure and the public comes in droves, but nevertheless the Dalí in decline, together with his paranoiac-critical method, did met with criticism. […] What is the fascination that makes visitors stand in queues? Probably not the seedy Dalí of the last 30 or 40 years, for whom the second half of a comprehensive retrospective would reserve a fate truly worthy of Dante. […] Picasso could become a myth for his day because he preserved an endless delicacy and an endless sympathy with life behind all the shocking brutality with which he handled reality. In Dalí do we detect a need for such identification or such sympathy?
1980

LUIS BUÑUEL
*Friend and film-maker*

Picasso was a painter and only a painter. Dalí went well beyond that. Certain sides to his character are dreadful - his passion for self-publicity, his exhibitionism, his strained efforts to be original in his gestures and his utterances, […] but in spite of all that he is an authentic, incomparable genius, writer, conversationalist and thinker. We were close friends for a long time and our collaboration on the screenplay for 'Un chien andalou' has left me with a wonderful memory of being completely at one in our inclinations.
1983

WIELAND SCHMIED
*Art historian*

Dalí's secret was never to keep his secret life secret, but from his early years to make every effort to publicise it in all its aspects and as a result it has remained a secret to many people. Dalí the exhibitionist is of course not one of the least known but possibly still one of the least understood artists of our age. All the monstrous details he revealed to us with cynical frankness have on the whole damaged retrospective thinking about Dalí the phenomenon, because it was they that captured our attention.
1989

ERNST FUCHS
*Friend*

Salvador Dalí's appearance was always a magnificent gesture but friends and connoisseurs of his personality could detect a glittering spark of knowing self-mockery. This earned him the respect which his deep modesty deserved, a modesty which he bashfully disguised when he announced with self-assurance: 'I am a genius!' Anger and remorse were as foreign to him as was flaunting his modesty.
2001

# Index